D0086593

Martin Luther King, Jr.

Recent Titles in
Bibliographies and Indexes in Afro-American and African Studies

Black-Jewish Relations in the United States: A Selected Bibliography
Lenwood G. Davis, compiler

Black Immigration and Ethnicity in the United States:
An Annotated Bibliography
Center for Afroamerican and African Studies, The University of Michigan

Blacks in the American Armed Forces, 1776-1983: A Bibliography
Lenwood G. Davis and George Hill, compilers

Education of the Black Adult in the United States: An Annotated Bibliography
Leo McGee and Harvey G. Neufeldt, compilers

A Guide to the Archives of Hampton Institute
Fritz J. Malval, compiler

A Bibliographical Guide to Black Studies Programs in the United States:
An Annotated Bibliography
Lenwood G. Davis and George Hill, compilers

Wole Soyinka: A Bibliography of Primary and Secondary Sources
James Gibbs, Ketu H. Katrak, and Henry Louis Gates, Jr., compilers

Afro-American Demography and Urban Issues: A Bibliography
R. A. Obudho and Jeannine B. Scott, compilers

Afro-American Reference: An Annotated Bibliography of Selected Resources
Nathaniel Davis, compiler and editor

The Afro-American Short Story: A Comprehensive, Annotated Index
with Selected Commentaries
Preston M. Yancy, compiler

Black Labor in America, 1865-1983: A Selected Annotated Bibliography
Joseph Wilson, compiler and editor

Martin Luther King, Jr.

An Annotated Bibliography

Compiled by
Sherman E. Pyatt

Bibliographies and Indexes in Afro-American and African Studies, Number 12

Greenwood Press
New York • Westport, Connecticut • London

Library of Congress Cataloging-in-Publication Data

Pyatt, Sherman E.
Martin Luther King, Jr. : an annotated bibliography.

(Bibliographies and indexes in Afro-American and African studies, ISSN 0742-6925 ; no. 12)
Includes index.
1. King, Martin Luther—Bibliography. I. Title. II. Series.
Z8464.44.P9 1986 016.3234'092'4 86-7593
[E185.97.K5]
ISBN 0-313-24635-1 (lib. bdg. : alk. paper)

Library of Congress Catalog Card Number: 86-7593
ISBN: 0-313-24635-1
ISSN: 0742-6925

First published in 1986

Greenwood Press, Inc.
88 Post Road West, Westport, Connecticut 06881

Printed in the United States of America

The paper used in this book complies with the Permanent Paper Standard issued by the National Information Standards Organization (Z39.48-1984).

10 9 8 7 6 5 4 3 2 1

To Marilyn, Sean, Shomari, and Jacob Murray

Contents

Preface

Martin Luther King, Jr. must be considered one of the most important civil rights leaders of our time. There is no way of mentioning the civil rights movement without referring to him. Moreover, he was recognized as a renowned minister and scholar. Dr. King left an abundance of speeches, sermons, books, articles, and interviews.

His main purpose in life was to acquire equal rights for all people. He evoked praise and criticism from blacks and whites. Some contended that his philosophy inspired violence and disrespect for the law, while others believed that his ideology was too passive to bring about any significant changes in our society.

King preached a philosophy of nonviolence and civil disobedience, which led to numerous marches, rallies, and demonstrations. His actions were greatly responsible for ending many voting irregularities in the South, improving fair housing conditions, abolishing segregated public facilities, and the passage of the Civil Rights Acts.

Since his death, numerous commemorations and celebrations have been held in his honor. His life has inspired movies, the naming of streets, and buildings in his honor, and finally, a national holiday for his deeds in the field of civil and human rights. Dr. King will go down in American history as one of the most intriguing persons of the twentieth century.

The material presented in this work updates the 1977 work by William H. Fisher, Free At Last: A Bibliography of Martin Luther King, Jr. (Scarecrow Press). The present volume provides broader coverage of biographical sources and extensive references to remarks in the Congressional Record.

A major feature is the citations of declassified documents compiled by the Federal Bureau of Investigation (FBI) that detail surveillance on Dr. King from 1962 until the time of his death. These documents allow the researcher to examine King and his involvement with the civil rights movement. Many of these documents were secured illegally through the use of wiretaps and microphones that were secretly hidden in King's hotel rooms.

Many of these documents were considered too sensitive by the Justice Department and were placed in the National Archives until the year 2027. The remainder of these documents are housed at the FBI reading room in Washington, D. C. and are available on microfilm (Garrow, David J. ed. The Martin Luther King, Jr. FBI File. Frederick, MD: University Publications of America. 16 microfilm reels with printed guide.)

Through the use of computer literature searches, I was able to generate a large array of material by and about Dr. King; a total of almost thirteen hundred items were published over the thirty-year period, from 1955 to 1984. Included are close to 190 citations of works by King, many reprinted since his death in 1968, and some ninety biographical references.

Chapter 1 contains numerous references of books, articles, speeches, sermons, and interviews by King.

Chapter 2 includes material that covers the life of King from his early childhood to his death. Some entries are brief while others are quite in-depth.

Chapter 3 focuses on the activities and functions of the Southern Christian Leadership Conference and King's involvement with this organization.

Chapter 4 pertains to the numerous rallies, marches, and demonstrations that King participated in during his career as a civil rights leader. Reactions to these demonstrations by public and government officials are also included.

Chapter 5 includes information relating to reactions from various people on his being awarded the Nobel Prize and the several other awards he received during his lifetime.

Chapter 6 deals with government representatives who sought to discredit King as a civil rights leader. A large amount of the material in this chapter covers the FBI's attempt to discredit and harass King through the use of wiretaps, informants, and other tactics.

Chapter 7 contains material that seeks to critique and interpret some of the basic thoughts of King on various subjects.

Chapter 8 includes information that studies the circumstances involving the death of King, the effect his death had on various groups and on society as a whole, the several previous threats and attempts on his life, the assassin himself, and the notion that a conspiracy against King existed.

Chapter 9 contains materials on the numerous eulogies, tributes, memorials, and commemorations given in honor of King.

Author and subject indexes and a title index to King's own works complete the volume.

Each of the nine chapters is subdivided into sections listing books, articles, dissertations, and government documents, except for chapter 1, which follows a chronological sequence. Newspaper articles and foreign publications are omitted. An asterisk (*) identifies sources written for a juvenile audience.

Brief annotations are provided to assist the user in making selections. Some citations appear without annotations if the source was not personally examined or if the title is self-explanatory. Page references are provided for encyclopedic and dictionary-type works.

Many thanks to Herb Nath, Pearl Erickson, Barbara Secrest, and Gail Tolbert for their assistance with this work. I am especially indebted to the Citadel Development Foundation for making this project possible. Though many people assisted and encouraged me in this endeavor, I take full responsibility for any omissions or errors that appear in this bibliography.

It is my hope that this bibliography will serve as a valuable resource for those who study and appreciate the career and deeds of Dr. Martin Luther King, Jr., a scholar and a leader of the civil rights movement.

List of Abbreviations

Alabama Rev - Alabama Review
Am Educ - American Education
Am Herit - American Heritage
Am Hist Rev - American History Review
Am J Sociol - American Journal of Sociology
Am Libraries - American Libraries
Am Opinion - American Opinion
Am Q - American Quarterly
Antioch Rev - Antioch Review
Bapt Hist and Herit - Baptist History and Heritage
Beijing R - Beijing Review
Black Enterp - Black Enterprise
Bus Week - Business Week
Cath Mess - Catholic Messenger
Center for Child Bks Bull - Center for Children Books Bulletin
Child Today - Children Today
Christ Century - Christian Century
Christ Sci Mon - Christian Science Monitor
Christ and Crisis - Christianity and Crisis
Christ Today - Christianity Today
Civ Lib Rev - Civil Liberties Review
Coll Comp and Comm - College Computers and Communication
Comm Educ - Communative Education
Comp and Auto - Computers and Automation
Comp and People - Computers and People
Cong QW Rept - Congressional Quarterly Weekly Report
Cong Rec - Congressional Record
Cont Rev - Contempory Review
Cont Soc - Contempory Sociology
DAI - Dissertation Abstracts International
Devel Psychol - Developmental Psychology
Econ Justice - Economic Justice
Edit Res Rep - Editorial Research Reports
Educ Dig - Education Digest
El Eng - Elementary English
Eng Jnl - English Journal
Gandhi Mag - Gandhi Magazine
Horn Bk - Horn Books
Interracial Rev - Interracial Review
J of Am Hist - Journal of American History

J Black Stud - Journal of Black Studies
J Current Soc Issues - Journal of Current Social Issues
J Ethnic Stud - Journal of Ethnic Studies
J Hist Ideas - Journal of History of Ideas
J Hum Rel - Journal of Human Relations
J Negro Hist - Journal of Negro History
J Pol - Journal of Politics
J Rel Thought - Journal of Religious Thought
J Soc Issues - Journal of Social Issues
J South Hist - Journal of Southern History
Kirkus Rev - Kirkus Review
Library J - Library Journal
Mass Rev - Massachusetts Review
Midwest Q - Midwest Quarterly
Min of One - Minority of One
Natl Rev - National Review
Negro Educ R - Negro Educational Review
Negro Hist Bull - Negro History Bulletin
New Repub - New Republic
NY Herald Trib Bk Rev - New York Herald Tribune Book Review
NY Rev Bks - New York Review of Books
NY State Ed - New York State Board of Education
NY Times book Rev - New York Times Book Review
NY Times Mag - New York Times Magazine
NJEA Rev - NJEA Review
Pol Sci Q - Political Science Quarterly
Pop Photogr - Popular Photography
Pop Sci - Popular Science
Presb Life - Presbyterian Life
Presb Outlook - Presbyterian Outlook
Psychol Today - Psychology Today
Pub Opinion Q - Public Opinion Quarterly
Ramp Mag - Ramparts Magazine
Read Dig - Reader's Digest
Rel Studies Rev - Religious Studies Review
Rev Black Pol Econ - Review of lack Political Economy
Saturday Rev - Saturday Review
Sch Lib J - School Library Journal
Sch Mgt - School Management
Sr Schol - Senior Scholastic
Soc Educ - Social Education
Soc Forces - Social Forces
Soc Order - Social Order
South Atlantic Q - South Atlantic Quarterly
South Expo - Southern Exposure
South Sch News - Southern School News
Spec - Spectrum
Theol Today - Theology Today
Times Lit Supp - Times Literary Supplement
US News World Rept - U.S. News & World Report
UNESCO Cour - UNESCO Courier
USA Today - USA Today
Va Q Rev - Virginia Quarterly Review
W Comp Pres Docs - Weekly Compilation of Presidential Documents
Wis Lib Bul - Wilson Library Bulletin

Martin Luther King, Jr.

Published Works By Martin Luther King, Jr. (1955-1984)

1955

0001 King, Martin Luther. "A Comparison of the Conceptions of God in the Thinking of Paul Tillich and Henry Nelson Wieman." Boston University, DAI, 1955, 19: 1458-A.

1956

0002 "Our Struggle." Liberation, Vol. 1, April, 1956, pp. 3-6.

Addresses the institution of segregation and the significance of the boycott in Montgomery.

0003 "Walk for Freedom." Fellowship, Vol. 22, May, 1956, p. 5.

0004 "The New Negro of the South." Socialist Call, Vol. 23, June, 1956, pp. 16-19.

An overall view of the Negro attitude regarding race relations, and what can be done to make it better.

0005 Bennett, Lerone, Jr. "The King Plan for Freedom." Ebony, Vol. II, July, 1956, pp. 65-69.

King outlines eight major points that can bring segregation to an end in America.

0006 King, M. L. "Alabama's Bus Boycott: What It's all About." US News World Rep, Vol. 41, August 3, 1956, pp. 82-89.

Discusses the bus boycott and the ongoing struggle by blacks for equality and justice in American society.

0007 "We are Still Walking." Liberation, Vol. 1, December, 1956, pp. 6-9.

Examines the continuous legalities after the court rules against segregation buses in Montgomery.

0008 Not Used.

1957

0009 "Nonviolence and Racial Justice." Christ Century, Vol. 74, February 6, 1957, pp. 165-167.

Contends that through the use of effective nonviolent resistance oppressed people can conquer the social evils that exist.

0010 "Facing the Challenge of a New Age." Phylon Q, Vol. 18, April, 1957, pp. 25-34.

Elaborates on several key issues that are essential to bringing about freedom and respect for blacks.

0011 Jack, Homer A. "Conversation in Ghana." Christ Century, Vol. 74, April 10, 1957, pp. 446-48.

King talks about certain aspects of segregation, violence and freedom while visiting Ghana.

0012 "A View of the Dawn." Interracial Rev, Vol. 30, May 1957, pp. 82-85.

An excerpt of King's address after accepting the Social Justice Award.

0013 "Civil Rights Bill Moves to Fore." Christ Century, Vol. 64, June 5, 1957, p. 700.

Urges the President of the United States and Congress to pass the Civil Rights Bill and allow blacks the right to vote.

0014 "The Most Durable Power." Christ Century, Vol. 74, June 5, 1957, p. 708.

Addresses the use of love as a means of achieving social and racial justice.

0015 "At the Threshold of Integration." Econ Justice, Vol. 24, June-July, 1957, p. 1.

1958

0016 "Nonviolence; The Christian Way in Human Relations." Presb Life, Vol. 2, February 8, 1958, p. 11.

0017 "Out of the Long Night of Segregation." Presb Outlook, Vol. 140, February 10, 1958, p. 6.

0018 "A Negro and Negroes." Newsweek, Vol. 51, February 24, 1958, p. 32.

Addresses some of the problems that blacks should correct before they can expect to be accepted by whites.

0019 King, Martin Luther, Jr. "The Current Crisis in Race Relations." New South, Vol. 13, March, 1958, pp. 8-12.

Explains the problems of race relations in the South and what can be done to correct these problems.

0020 "Who Speaks for the South?" Liberation, Vol. 3, March, 1958, pp. 13-14.

Observations are made concerning blacks in the South and their continuous battle for the right to vote.

0021 "The Power of Nonviolence." Intercollegian, Vol. 75, May, 1958, pp. 8-9.

Discusses the background of the Montgomery boycott and the use of nonviolence in accomplishing their goals.

0022 "An Experiment in Love." Jubilee, Vol. 6, September, 1958, pp. 11-17.

Details the events of the Montgomery bus boycott and explains King's philosophy of nonviolence and love as a tool for accomplishing goals.

0023 "The Church and the Race Crisis." Christ Century, Vol. 65, October 8, 1958, pp. 1140-41.

The church faces a moral obligation to try and eliminate racial segregation.

1959

0024 "The Social Organization of Non-violence." Liberation, Vol. 4, October, 1959, pp. 5-6.

Gives reasons for the use of nonviolence as a means for gáining civil rights as compared to using the method of violence.

0025 "My Trip to the Land of Gandhi." Ebony, Vol. 14, July, 1959, pp. 84-86, 88-90, 92.

Recalls the events and activities that took place on his visit to India.

1960

0026 "King Announces Plan to Move to Atlanta." South Sch News, Vol. 6, January, 1960, p. 9.

King feels that the move to Atlanta would present a better base of operations for SCLC. Also, he comments on the legal battle surrounding the closing of segregated parks.

0027 "Full-Scale Assalt." Newsweek, Vol. 55, February 29, 1960, pp. 24-25.

Discusses the form of protest that should be used to wipe out segregation.

0028 "Revolt without Violence -- the Negroes' New Strategy." US News World Rep, Vol. 48, March 21, 1960, pp. 76-78.

An extensive interview with Dr. King discussing his views on what can be done to bring about full citizenship rights for blacks in the U.S.

0029 "Pilgrimage to Non-Violence." Christ Century, Vol. 77, April 13, 1960, pp. 439-441.

Views his theological teaching and the circumstances that led to his practice of nonviolence.

0030 "Suffering and Faith." Christ Century, Vol. 77, April 27, 1960, p. 510.

Talks about his philosophy of suffering and his relationship with God.

0031 "The Burning Truth in the South." Progressive, Vol. 24, May, 1960, pp. 8-10.

Examines the black students' use of sit-down protest to achieve equal justice with whites.

0032 "The Rising Tide of Racial Consciousness." YWCA, Magazine, Vol. 54, December, 1960, pp. 4-6.

Discusses the factors that brought a sense of pride and self respect for blacks and his fight to gain first-class citizenship in America.

1961

0033 "Equality Now." Nation, Vol. 192, February 4, 1961, pp. 91-95.

Calls on Congress and the President to bring about changes in the social, political and economic aspects of blacks in America.

0034 "The Man Who Was a Fool." The Pulpit, Vol. 32, June, 1961, p. 4.

0035 "'Time for Freedom Has Come!'" NY Times Mag, September 10, 1961, pp. 25, 118-119.

King comments on the youths' and students' involvement in the Civil Rights struggle.

0036 "Love, Law and Civil Disobedience." New South, Vol. 16, December, 1961, pp. 3-11.

Addresses the ideals and principles of the student movement and the racial crisis that exists in America.

0037 Bradford, D. "Martin Luther King Says: "I'd Do It All Again." Sepia, Vol. 10, December, 1961, pp. 15-19.

1962

0038 Fey, Harold E. The Christian Century Reader: Representative Articles, Editorials, and Poems Selected from More Than Fifty Years of the Christian Century. New York: Association Press, 1962.

Dr. King elaborates on his theory of nonviolence and racial justice.

0039 "We Shall Overcome." IUD Digest, Vol. 7, Spring, 1962, pp. 19-27.

Compares the problems and needs of the labor movement with that of the civil rights movement.

0040 "A Legacy of Creative Protest." Mass Rev, Vol. 4, Autumn, 1962, p. 43.

Reveals the impact of Thoreau's writing on King, which led to his practice in civil disobedience.

0041 "Fumbling on the New Frontier." Nation, Vol. 194, March 3, 1962, pp. 190-193.

Comments on several actions that the Kennedy administration should act upon to bring about better racial equaity in America.

0042 "Hate is Always Tragic; Martin Luther King's Challenge." Time, Vol. 80, August 3, 1962, p. 13.

Covers excerpts of King's philosophy on nonviolent resistance.

0043 "The Case Against 'Tokenism.'" NY Times Mag, August 5, 1962, pp. 11, 49, 52-53.

Addresses the problems that exist for blacks and what changes should be made to bring about racial equality.

0044 "Who Is Their God?" Nation, Vol. 195, October 13, 1952, pp. 209-210.

Covers the events that have taken place in Mississippi during the desegregation fight of one of its colleges.

1963

0045 Weinberg, Arthur and Lila, eds. Instead of Violence, Writings by the Great Advocates of Peace and Nonviolence Throughout History. New York: Grossman Publishers, 1963.

King gives an historical account of his philosophy on nonviolence.

0046 Davis, Jerome. World Leaders I Have Known. New York: Citadel Press, 1963.

King expresses his views on the theory of pacifism, and his feelings on what role the church can play in ending racial injustice in the South.

0047 King, Martin Luther, Jr. Strength to Love. New York: Harper & Row, Publishers, 1963.

A group of sermons preached during the time of the Montgomery bus boycott and dealing with the social problems during that time period.

0048 "Bold Design for a new South." Nation, Vol. 196, March 30, 1963, pp. 259-262.

Blames the President and his administration for the problems that came about with the struggle for civil rights.

0049 "The Ethical Demands of Integration - A Philosophy of Race Relations." Religion and Labor, Vol. 6, May, 1963, pp. 1-8.

Dr. King gives his views on integration and what methods that can be utilized to achieve this ultimate goal.

0050 Rose, S. C. "Test for Nonviolence." Christ Century, Vol. 80, May 29, 1963, pp. 714-716.

King gives his reasons for protesting and demonstrating and expains why he feels his methods of nonviolence will help to end racial segregation in the U.S.

0051 King, Martin Luther, Jr. "Letter from a Birmingham Jail." Liberation, Vol. 8, June, 1963, pp. 10-11+

0052 Not Used.

0053 "Letter from a Birmingham Jail." Christ Century, Vol. 80, June 12, 1963, pp. 767-773.

The letter in its entirety is presented in response to critism expressed by eight clergymen.

0054 "Letter from a Birmingham City Jail: Wait Almost Always Means Never." New Leader, Vol. 46, June 24, 1963, pp. 3-11.

Includes the text of the statement by eight clergymen asking King to withdraw from demonstrations in Birmingham.

0055 "Letter from the Birmingham City Jail." Interracial Rev, Vol. 36, July, 1963, p. 150-155.

0056 "Love and Nonviolence and the Shame of Segregation." Jubilee, Vol. 11, July, 1963, pp. 22-23.

Strongly believes that the injustices of segregation can only be eradicated by nonviolent protests and demonstrations.

0057 "Why the Negro Won't Wait." Financial Post, Vol. 57, July 27, 1963, p. 6.

0058 "A Letter from Birmingham Jail." Ebony, Vol. 18, August, 1963 pp. 23-26, 28, 30, 32-33.

0059 "The Negro is Your Brother." Atlantic Monthly, Vol. 207, August, 1963, pp. 78-81, 86-88.

While imprisoned in Birmingham, King answers critics about his involvment in the civil rights movement.

0060 "Is It All Right to Break the Law?" US News World Rep, Vol. 55, August 12, 1963, p. 6

Contends that it is acceptable to break laws that are felt to be unjust.

0061 "200,00 Join in Orderly Civil Rights March on Washington." Cong Q W Rept, Vol. 21, August 30, 1963, pp. 1495-6+.

Dr. King's statements on what he hoped the march would accomplish are mentioned.

0062 Long, Margaret. "March on Washington." New South, Vol. 18, September, 1963, pp. 3-19.

Excerpts of King's "I Have A Dream" speech are given.

0063 "Dream, I Have a Dream: Excerpts From an Address to Washington Marchers." Newsweek, Vol. 62, September 9, 1963, p. 21.

Expresses a hope that people of all colors will be able to live together without hate and violence.

0064 "In a Word: Now." NY Times Mag, September 29, 1963, pp. 91-92.

Expresses the demands and needs of blacks in America.

0065 "Action for Interracial Understanding." Franciscan Herald and Forum, Vol. 42, October, 1963, p. 289.

King outlines seven principles that should be used to bring about racial harmony.

0066 "M.L.K." Catholic Worker, Vol. 30, October, 1963, p. 7.

Contains an excerpt from King's book, Strength to Love.

0067 "Back on the Home Front." Time, Vol. 82, December 27, 1963, p. 17.

King addresses the segregation laws in Atlanta.

0068 U.S. Congress, Senate. Senator Javits speaking for "March on Washington." 89th Cong., 1st Sess., Cong Rec, Vol. 109, September 3, 1963, S16240-16242.

King's "I Have a Dream Speech" is included in its entirety.

0069 U.S. Congress, Senate. Senator Douglas speaking for "The March on Washington." 89th Cong., 1st Sess., Cong Rec, Vol. 109, September 3, 1963, S116227-16232.

Includes an insert of King's "I Have a Dream" speech.

0070 FBI Headquarters Files. Rev. Martin Luther King, Jr. - Racial Matters. June 11, 1963, Washington, D.C.: FBI Headquarters Murkin Security Files, 2 p. (Mem. No. 145).

Initial plans are discussed by King and other members regarding the mass March on Washington.

0071 FBI Headquarters Files. Martin Luther King and the March on Washington. August 29, 1963, Washington, D.C.: FBI Headquarters Murkin Security Files, 3 p. (Mem. No. 205).

King addresses a conference in order to obtain ideas as to how to dramatize the proposed March on Washington.

1964

0072 Why We Can't Wait. New York: Harper & Row Publishers, 1964.

King reveals his reasoning for demonstrations and marches focusing on the Birmingham marches and the March on Washington.

0073 Westin, Alan F., ed. Freedom Now: The Civil-Rights Struggle in America. New York: Basic Books, Inc., Publishers, 1964.

In Part 1 the text of King's "Letter from Birmingham Jail" is given, and King expresses his views on several issues involving the civil rights movement.

0074 Clayton, Edward, ed. The SCLC Story in Words and Pictures. Atlanta: The Southern Christian Leadership Conference, 1964.

A copy of King's speech "I Have a Dream" is presented.

0075 Wish, H., ed. The Negro Since Emancipation. New Jersey: Prentice-Hall, Inc., 964.

Pages 158-157 contain a reprint of a chapter from King's book Stride Toward Freedom dealing with the decision to go ahead with the bus boycott.

0076 Daniel, B., ed. Black, White, and Gray: Twenty-One Points of View on the Race Question. New York: Sheed and Ward, Inc., 1964.

Includes a copy of "Letter from Birmingham's Jail."

0077 "Letter from a Birmingham Jail." Time, Vol. 83, January 3, 1964, p. 15.

0078 "Boycotts Will Be Used." US News World Rep, Vol. 56, February 24, 1964, pp. 59-61.

States that there could be increased protest and demonstrations if the Civil Rights Bill is not passed in Congress.

0079 "Letter from a Birmingham Jail." Negro Hist Bull, Vol. 27, March, 1964, p. 156.

A reprint from Time magazine of excerpts from the letter written by King.

0080 "Hammer of Civil Rights." Nation, Vol. 198, March 9, 1964, pp. 230-34.

Addresses the technique of nonviolent action as a means of obtaining equal justice and civil rights.

0081 "Why We Can't Wait; Excerpts." Life, Vol. 56, May 15, 1964, pp. 98-100, 101-102, 104, 107-108, 110, 112.

Interprets the idea of freedom for blacks in America.

0082 "Why We Can't Wait; Excerpts." Saturday Rev, Vol. 47, May 30, 1964, pp. 17-20, 76.

Contains a preview from King's book Why We Can't Wait.

0083 "The Sword That Heals." Critic, Vol. 22, June-July 1964, pp. 6-14.

Examines social, historical, and psychological conditions that brought about the civil rights movement and the circumstances that established the idea of nonviolent action.

0084 "No Man's Land; St. Augustine, Fla." Newsweek, Vol. 64, July 6, 1964, pp. 16-17.

King comments on the lack of protection for demonstrators in St. Augustine.

0085 King, Martin Luther, Jr. "Nonviolence, the Only Way." Indo-Asian Culture, Vol. 13, October, 1964, pp. 54-62.

Dr. King explains his philosophy of passive resistance ad tells why he feels this is the best weapon to fight against racial injustice.

0086 "Negroes Are Not Moving Too Fast." Saturday Evening Post, Vol. 237,. November 7, 1964, pp. 8, 10.

Addresses several myths about blacks and their fight for civil rights and social justice.

0087 "It's a Difficult Thing to Teach a President." Look, Vol. 28, November 17, 1964, pp. 61, 64.

King discusses his relationship with President Kennedy in regards to the civil rights movement.

0088 "Martin Luther King's Reaction - a Statement and a Disagreement." US News World Rep, Vol. 57, November 30, 1964, p. 58.

Comments on remarks that were made about him by the FBI Director.

0089 "Two Perspectives, One Goal." Time, Vol. 84, December 18, 1964, pp. 21-22.

Talks about a brighter future for America in regard to solving the problem of race relations.

0090 FBI Headquarters Files. Rev. Martin Luther King, Jr. Appearance on "Face the Nation" Sunday, May 10, 1964, 12:30 p.m., Channel 9, WTOP-TV. May 1, 1964, Washington, D.C.: FBI Headquarters Murkin Security Files, 2 p. (Mem. No. 361).

King talks in great length about Communism and civil rights.

0091 FBI Headquarters Files. Talks by Rev. Martin Luther King, Jr. at San Diego State College and California Western University, San Diego, California on May 29, 1964. June, 1964, Washington, D.C.: FBI Headquarters Murkin Security Files, 2 p. (Men no. 371).

King speaks against segregation in the U.S. and urges that the Civil Rights Bill be passed.

0092 FBI Headquarters File. CP, USA Negro Question Communist Influence in Racial Matters. June 16, 1964, Washington, D.C.: FBI Headquarters Murkin Security Files, 10 p. (Int. Sec. No. 414).

King addresses the National Convention of the Republican Party on the subject of discrimination and segregation.

0093 FBI Headquarters Files. Communist Party, United States of America - Negro Question. June 26, 1964, Washington, D.C.: FBI Headquarters Murkin Security Files, 2 p. (Mem. No. N/A).

King talks about the violent attacks on the demonstrators in St. Augustine, Florida, and his plans to bring these attacks to an end.

1965

0094 Broderick, F. L. and Meier, A., eds. Negro Protest Thought in the Twentieth Century. Indianapolis: The Bobbs-Merrill, Co., 1965.

Includes a reprinted a exerpt of Dr. King's book, Stride Toward Freedom, and a reprint of his "I Have a Dream" speech.

0094 Not Used.

0096 King, Martin, Luther, Jr. Martin Luther King, Jr., Recipient of the 1964 Nobel Peace Prize, Oslo, Norway, December 11, 1964. New York: Harper & Row, 1965.

Addresses the topic of civil rights for blacks and the eradication of poverty in America.

0097 "Dr. King Accepts." Crisis, Vol. 72, January, 1965, p. 8.

0098 "Civil Right No. 1 -- The Right to Vote." NY Time Mag, March 14, 1965, pp. 26-7, 94-95.

The disfranchisement of blacks in the South is discussed.

0099 "'Let Justice Roll Down'." Nation, Vol. 200, March 15, 1965, pp. 269-274.

King talks about the progress of the civil rights movement and the events that took place in Alabama.

0100 "'Dreams of Brighter Tomorrows'." Ebony, Vol. 20, March, 1965. pp. 34-35.

Comments on what the Nobel Peace Prize symbolizes to hime and the civil rights movement.

0101 "Selma - the Shame and the Promise: the Negroes' Fight for Voting Rights and Human Dignity." IUD Agenda, Vol. I, March, 1965, pp. 18-21.

Addresses the historical and legal difficulties of blacks attempting to vote in Selma.

0102 "Behind the Selma March." Saturday Rev, Vol. 48, April 3, 1965, pp. 16-17+.

Elaborates and outlines the background of the events that led to the march in Selma.

0103 "Road from Selma: Hope -- and Death." Newsweek, Vol. 65, April 5, 1965, pp. 23-28.

Excerpts of Dr. King's speech during the march to Montgomery.

0104 "King." New Yorker, Vol. 41, May 1, 1965, pp. 35-37.

King addresses a group of lawyers on the subject of law and morality.

0105 "The Un-Christian Christian; SCLC Leader looks Closely at Christianity in Troubled Land." Ebony, Vol. 20, August, 1965, pp. 76-80.

Examines the true nature of the Christian that portrays the attitude of apathy and indifference toward the social injustices in America.

0106 "Dr. King and the Paris Press." America, Vol. 113, November 13, 1965, p. 560.

King addresses an audience in Paris on his philosophy of nonviolence.

0107 "Next Stop: the North." Saturday Rev, Vol. 48, November 13, 1965, pp. 33-35, 105.

Explores the outcomes of demonstrations in the South to those of the North and explains the reasons that violence was a major problem in the North.

0108 U.S. Congress, House. Representative Frank Thompson remarks on "What Selma Is All About." 89th Cong., 1st Cong Rec, Vol. 111, March 15, 1965, pp. A1176-1172.

Contains an article written by King entitled, "Civil Rights No. 1 -- The Right to Vote."

0109 FBI Headquarters Files. Martin Luther King, Jr. Partcipates in a Panel Discussion. May 6, 1965, Washington, D.C.: FBI Headquarters Murkin Security Files, 6 p. (Encl. No. 1325).

King expresses his views on several topics involving civil rights and equal justice for blacks.

0110 FBI Headquarters Files. King Holds a News Conference in Chicago. July 7, 1965, Washington, D.C.: FBI Headquarters Murkin Security Files, 3 p. (Tel. No. 1547).

States that he and SCLC are in Chicago to begin their fight for integrated education for the children of Chicago.

0111 FBI Headquarters Files. Martin Luther King, Jr. Arrives in Chicago. July 8, 1985, Washington, D.C.: FBI Headquarters Murkin Security Files, 4 p. (Encl. No. 1563).

Contains a copy of King's press conference release which explains his reasons for bringing his civil rights movement to the North.

0112 FBI Headquarters files. Proposed Letters From King to President Johnson. September 15, 1965, Washington, D.C.: FBI Headquarters Murkin Security Files, 2 p. (Corr. No. 1866).

King discusses with his advisors the steps he should take to curtail the criticisms against him because of his stance on the Vietnam War.

1966

0113 Lynd, S., ed. Nonviolence in America: A Documentary History. Indianapolis: The Bobbs-Merrill Co., Inc., 1966.

Contains a reprinted copy of "Letter from Birmingham City Jail."

0114 Handy, Robert T., ed. The Social Gospel in America. New York: Oxford University Press, 1966.

King expresses his views on a book written by Rauschenbusch and the impact it had on his philosophy and way of thinking.

0115 "Freedom's Crisis: Last Steep Ascent." Nation, Vol. 202, March 14, 1966, p. 288.

0116 Wilkins, R. "Negro Leaders Dividing: The Effect." US News World Rept, Vol. 61, July 18, 1966, pp. 31-34.

King expresses his views on the ideology of black power.

0117 King, Jr. "Nonviolence: The Only Road to Freedom." Ebony, Vol. 21, October, 1966, pp. 27-30+.

Concludes that through the use of nonviolence blacks can obtain the social justice and equality they deserve.

0118 "Doctor King's Case for Nonviolence." America, Vol. 115, November 12, 1966, p. 578.

Dr. King takes his stance on nonviolence and explains how peace can be achieved through its use.

0119 "Gift of Love." McCalls, Vol. 94, December, 1966, p. 146.

0120 FBI Headquarters Files. Statement by Martin Luther King, Jr., President, SCLC, Chicago, Illinois. January 10, 1966, Washington, D.C.: FBI Headquarters Murkin Security Files, 14 p. (Airtel No. 2206).

King explains the problems that he sees facing the North and outlines the remedies that can be used to solve them.

1967

0121 Franklin, John Hope, and Starr, Isidore, eds. The Negro in Twentieth Century America. New York: Random House, Vintage Books, 1967.

Includes King's "I Have a Dream" speech and "Letter from Birmingham City Jail."

0122 The Trumpet of Conscience. New York: Harper & Row Publishers, 1967.

Discusses his views on the war in Vietnam, his ideology of nonviolence, and his desire for world peace.

0123 Where Do We Go from Here: Chaos or Community? New York: Harper & Row Publishers, 1967.

Addresses the problems that must be looked at in order to achieve equality for black people.

0124 "Lord of the Doves." Newsweek, Vol. 69, April 17, 1967, pp. 44-46.

King calls for an end to the war in Vietnam; he feels that the U.S. is on the road to colonization.

0125 "Doctor King's Crusade: How He Hopes to End the War." US News World Rept, Vol. 62, May 8, 1967, p. 14.

King announces plans to organize a movement that would fight for ending the war in Vietnam.

0126 King, Martin Luther. "Declaration of Independence from the War in Vietnam." Ramparts, Vol. 5, May, 1967, pp. 32-37.

Asks America to make an effort to end the war in Vietnam through negotiations.

0127 "A New Kind of Power." Progressive, June 1967, pp. 13-17.

Defines and analyzes the ideology of black power.

0128 "Martin Luther King Explains." Negro Digest, Vol. 16, June, 1967, pp. 5-7.

The opposition to America's fighting in Vietnam is discussed in this article.

0129 "Martin Luther King Defines 'Black Power'." NY Times Mag, Vol. 11, June 26, 1967.

0130 "Cities in '68." New Repub, Vol. 157, December 16, 1967, pp. 5-7.

Dr. King outlines his plans and reasons for staging a march on Washington.

0131 U.S. Congress, House. Representative Edwards speaking for "Dr. Martin Luther King on Vietnam." 90th Cong., 1st Sess., Cong Rec, Vol. 113, May 2, 1967, pp. H11402-11406.

Contains a reprint of an article expressing the views of Dr. King on the subject of Vietnam.

1968

0132 Adoff, A., ed. Black on Black: Commentaries by Negro Americans. New York: MacMillan Co., 1968.

A reprint copy of "Letter from Birmingham Jail" is presented in this volume.

0133 Blaustein, A. I. and Woock, R. R., eds. Man Against Poverty: World War III. New York: Random House, Inc., 968.

King attempts to explain the birth and justifications of black power in this volume.

0134 Cunningham, George J. Poor Black People. Michigan: Sherwood Forest Pubs., 1968.

Includes excerpts of several of Dr. King's speeches and statements.

0135 Goldwin, Robert A., ed. Civil Disobedience; Five Essays. Ohio: Public Affairs Conference Center, 1968.

King addresses the subject of civil disobedience through a letter he wrote while in jail.

0136 Harrison, Deloris. We Shall Live in Peace: The Teachings of Martin Luther King, Jr. New York: Hawthorn Books, Inc., 1968.

0137 Hoskins, Lotte, ed. "I Have a Dream;" The Quotations of Martin Luther King, Jr. New York: Grosset & Dunlap, 1968.

Explores the various social issues that King addressed during his lifetime.

0138 Lowi, T. J., ed. Private Life and Public Order. New York: W. W. Norton and Co., Inc., 1968.

Part 1 contains a copy of King's "Letter from Birmingham Jail."

0139 Wechman, Robert J., comp. Readings and Interpretations of Critical Issues in Modern American Life. New York: Selected Academic Readings, 1968.

Contains a copy of King's letter written while he was being held in a Birmingham jail cell.

0140 The Trumpet of Conscience. New York: Harper & Row Publishers, 1968.

Discusses nonviolent protests, our role in Vietnam, and several other subjects of concern during the 1960s.

0141 "The Role of the Behavioral Scientist in the Civil Rights Movement." J Soc Issues, Vol. 24, January, 1968, pp. 1-12.

King talks about the role of social scientists and what they can do to assist the civil rights movement.

0142 Yglesias, Jose. "Doctor King's March on Washington, Part 2." NY Times Mag, March 31, 1968, pp. 30-31+.

King discusses two major problems that were facing Americans at that time.

0143 King, M. L. "Showdown for Nonviolence." Look, Vol. 32, April 16, 1968, pp. 23-24.

0144 "Living Legacy of Martin Luther King, Jr.; Excerpts from Addresses. Sr Schol, Vol. 92, April 25, 1968, p. 19.

Synopses of several of King's speeches given on various topics.

0145 "From the Birmingham Jail." Negro Hist Bull, Vol. 31, May, 1968, p. 19.

This excerpt gives reasons why blacks were not willing to wait any longer to end segregation and racial injustice.

0146 "I Have a Dream" Negro Hist Bull, Vol. 31, May, 1968, pp. 16-18.

0147 King, M. L. "America's Racial Crisis." Curr, Vol. 95, May, 1968, pp. 6-10.

A campaign of nonviolent demonstrations to fight for the end of poverty in America is discussed.

0148 "Speeches by Dr. Martin Luther King, Jr." Negro Hist Bull, Vol. 31, May, 1968, p. 22.

Three of his speeches are given, including his last speech given in Memphis the day before he was killed.

0149 "Editorials from Newsletter." Negro Hist Bull, Vol. 31, May 1968, pp. 18-19.

Reveals the problems that he and SCLC encountered while demonstrating in St. Augustine, Fla., and assesses the achievement of the civil rights movement in 1963.

0150 "The American Dream." Negro Hist Bull, Vol. 31, 1968, pp. 10-13.

Addresses a graduating class on the social and economic conditions of America and what can be done to make them better.

0151 Not Used.

0152 "The Acceptance Speech of Martin Luther King, Jr. of the Nobel Peace Prize on December 10, 1964." Negro Hist Bull, Vol. 31, May, 1968, pp. 20-21.

0153 "Words of Martin Luther King, Jr. Can Live in the minds of Our Children." Instructor, Vol. 77, June, 1968, p. 17.

Contains an Excerpt from King's book, Strenght to Love.

0154 "Say That I Was A Drum Major." Read Digest, Vol. 92, June, 1968, p. 58.

Contains portions of a sermon delivered by King in Atlanta.

0155 FBI Headquarters Files. Washington Spring Project. March 20, 1968, Washington, D.C." FBI Headquarters Murkin Security Files, 5 p. (Tel., No. 3260).

King addresses a crowd in Jackson, Miss. about SCLC's plans for a Poor People's March on Washington.

0156 U.S. Congress, House. Representative Moorehead comments on "A

Medal in Honor of Martin Luther King, Jr." 90th Cong., 2nd Sess., Cong Rec, Vol. 114, April 8, 1968, pp. H9164-9165.

Contains the text of King's "I Have a Dream" speech.

0157 Not Used.

1969

0158 Thomas, William B., comp. Shall Not Perish. Nine Speeches by Three Great Americans. Denmark: Gyldendal, 1969.

King gives his philosophy of peace through his "I Have a Dream" speech and "Letter from a Birmingham Jail."

0159 Koch, Thilo. Fighters for a New World: John F. Kennedy, Martin Luther King, Robert F. Kennedy. New York: G. P. Putnam's Sons,

Excerpts from King's Nobel Peace Prize speech and "I Have a Dream" speech are discussed.

0160 "Martin Luther King: We Shall Overcome." Unesco Cour, Vol. 22, October, 1969, p. 20.

King expresses his views for the fight for racial equality through the use of nonviolence.

1970

0161 Graham, John, ed. Great American Speeches, 1898-1963. New York: Appleton-Century-Crofts, 1970.

Includes a copy of King's "I Have a Dream" speech.

0162 Rose, P. I., ed. Americans from Africa Vol. 2. New York: Atherton Press, Inc., 1970.

In Chapter 16 King discusses the idea of black Americans acquiring power and utilizing it in the political and economic arenas.

0163 Kelen, Emery. Fifty Voices of the Twentieth Century. New York: Lothrop, Lee, and Shepard, Co. 1970.

Contains excerpts from some of King's major speeches and statements.

0164 Ducas, G., ed. Great Documents in Black American History. New York: Praeger Pubs., 1970.

A copy of King's "Letter from Birmingham Jail" is included.

0165 Rose, P. I., ed. Americans from Arica Vol. 2. New York: Atherton Press, Inc., 1970.

A condensed version of Chapter 5 from King's book, Where Do We Go from Here is mentioned.

0166 Storing, Herbert J. What Country Have I? New York: St. Martin's Press, 1970.

A reprint of King's "Letter from Birmingham Jail" is given.

0167 Deutsch, S. E. and Howard, J., eds. Where It's At: Radical Perspective in Sociology. New York: Harper and Row Publishers, 1970.

A reprint of an article by Dr. King entitled, "The Role of the Behavioral Scientist" is discussed in Part 1 of this volume.

0168 Messner, Gerald, ed. Another View: To Be Back in America. New York: Harcourt, Brace and World, Inc., 1970.

King addresses the problems and solutions of the civil rights movement.

0169 "Dr. King to Mrs. Amy E. Spingarn and Reply." Crisis, Vol. 77, April, 1970, p. 155.

King expresses his appreciation and gratitude for being chosen as the recipient of the Spingarn Medal.

0170 King, Martin Luther. "Love Your Enemies." Jnl of Rel Thought, Vol. 27, Summer 1970, pp. 31-41.

Elaborates on the philosophy of love and its power to achieve social justice.

1971

0171 Johnson, Joseph A. The Soul of the Black Preacher. Philadelphia: United Church Press, 1971.

Contains several excerpts of King's speeches and statements addressing the subject of nonviolence.

0172 Lyons, Thomas T. Black Leadership in American History. California: Addison-Wesley Pub. Co., 1971.

An excerpt of King's "Letter from a Birmingham Jail" is included in Chapter 5.

0173 Bosmajian, Haig A. The Rhetoric of Nonverbal Communication. Illinois: Scott, Foresman, 1971.

Contains a speech by Dr. King on the subject of nonviolence and oppression.

0174 Ford, Nick A. Black Insights: Significant Literature by Black Americans - 1760 to the Present. Waltham, MA: Ginn, 1971.

Includes an excerpt from King's book, Where Do We Go from Here: Chaos or Community?

0175 O'Neill, Daniel J., comp. Speeches by Black Americans. California: Dickenson Pub. Co., 1971.

Two of King's speeches are given: "I Have a Dream" and "Nonviolence and Social Change."

0176 Knight, Jant M., ed. Three Assassinations: The Death of John and Robert Kennedy and Martin Luther King. New York: Facts on File, Inc., 1971.

Knight has included an excerpt copy of King's "I Have a Dream" speech.

0177 Kent, Edward. Revolution and the Rule of Law. Englewood Cliffs, N.J.: Prentice-Hall, 1971.

Contains "Letter from a Birmingham Jail" explaining his reasoning for civil disobedience.

0178 Holland, Dewitte, ed. Sermons in American History. Nashville, Tenn.: Parthenon Press, 1971.

A brief excerpt from King's book, Why We Can't Wait is given.

1975

0179 Worton, Stanley N. Freedom of Assembly and Petition. New Jersey: Hayden Book Co., 1975.

Contains a copy of the "Letter from a Birmingham Jail."

1978

0180 Lewis, David L. King; A Critical Biography. Chicago: University of Illinois Press, 1978.

Excerpts from several of King's speeches and statements are given.

0181 Hatch, Jane M. American Book of Days. New York: H. W. Wilson Co., 1978.

A copy of Dr. King's "I Have a Dream" speech is included in this volume.

1979

0182 "On Martin Luther King, Jr.; Symposium." Today's Educ, Vol. 68, November/December, 1979, pp. 58-68.

Contains excerpts from several of King's speeches and books.

0183 "Martin L. King's 'Letter from Birmingham Jail.'" Encore, Vol. 8, November 19, 1979, pp. 19-21.

0184 "The Words of Martin Luther King, Jr." Today's Educ, Vol. 68, November/December, 1979, pp. 58-64.

Excerpts from such topics as education, world peace, discrimination, and nonviolent resistance are discussed.

1981

0185 Steinberg, S. Seven Against Odds. New York: Vantage Press, Inc., 1981.

In Chapter 6 an excerpt of King's "I Have a Dream" speech is given.

0186 King, Martin Luther, Jr. "Letter from a Birmingham Jail." South Expo, Vol. 9, Spring, 1981, pp. 51-54.

A reprint of King's letter responding to a group of clergymen's statements about his demonstrating in Alabama.

1983

0187 King, Coretta Scott. The Words of Martin Luther King, Jr. New York: Newmarket Press, 1983.

Several of King's speeches and sermons on various subjects are presented in this concise work.

1984

0188 "Suffering and Faith." Christ Century, Vol. 101, July 4-11, 1984, p. 687.

King gives his philosophy on suffering and its connection with faith.

0189 U.S. Congress, House. Representative Edward J. Markey remarks on "Letter from a Birmingham Jail." 98th Cong. 2nd Sess., Cong Rec, Vol. 130, April 4, 1984, pp. E1441-1443.

Biographical

BOOKS

0190 Adams, Russell L. Great Negroes, Past and Present. Chicago: Afro-Am Publishing, Co. 1963.

A brief biographical sketch of King and his involvement in the civil rights movement is given.

0191 Adler, Bill, ed. The Wisdom of Martin Luther King, in His Own Words. New York: Lancer Books, 1968.

Contains partial biographical material on King.

0192 *Alico, Stella H. Benjamin Franklin: Martin Luther King, Jr. Connecticut: Pendulum Press, 1979.

Alico covers the life of Dr. King in the format of a comic strip.

0193 Allen, Harold C. Great Black Americans. West Haven, Conn.: Pendulum, 1971.

Pages 71 through 94 chronologs the life of Dr. King and his fight for racial equality for blacks in America.

0194 *Behrens, June. Martin Luther King, Jr.: The Story of a Dream: A Play. Chicago: Childrens Pr., 1979.

A brief two-act play depicting the struggle of Dr. King in his fight for civil rights.

0195 Bennett, Lerone, Jr. What Manner of Man. Chicago: Johnson Pub., 1964.

A biographical look at King covering personal interviews with King and friends that knew him well.

0196 Bishop, Jim. The Days of Martin Luther King, Jr. New York: G. P. Putnam's Sons, 1971.

This biographical work concentrates on King's assassination along with his rise in the civil rights movement.

0197 Bleiweiss, Robert M. Marching to Freedom; the Life of Martin King, Jr. New York: New American Library, 1968.

Brief overview of the life and death of Martin Luther King.

0198 Bontemps, Arna W. 100 Years of Negro Freedom. New York: Dodd, Mead & Co., 1961.

Comments on the personal life and accomplishments of Dr. King during the Montgomery boycott.

0199 Bowden, Henry Warner. Dictionary of American Religious Biography. Connecticut: Greenwood Press, 1977, pp. 243-245.

0200 Burnett, Hugh, ed. Face to Face. New York: Stein and Day Publishers, 1964.

King recalls his fight against racial prejudice as a boy and a man.

0201 Candee, Marjorie Dent, ed. Current Biography Yearbook. New York: H. W. Wilson Co., 1958.

Looks at the life of Dr. King up to the events of the Montgomery bus boycott.

0202 Clemens, Thomas C. Martin Luther King, Man of Peace. Washington, D.C.: U.S. Information Service, 1965.

0203 Curtis, C. J. Contemporary Protestant Thought. New York: Bruce Pubs, Co., 1970.

A brief chronology of King's life is given in Chapter 13.

0204 Davis, Jerome. World Leaders I Have Known. New York: Citadel Press, 1963.

Briefly accounts the life of King and his struggles for civil rights.

0205 Davis, Lenwood G. "I Have a Dream" . . . The Life and Times of Martin Luther King, Jr. Connecticut: Greenwood Pr., 1973.

A detailed biography of Dr. King up to the time of his assassination.

0206 *DeKay, James T. Meet Martin Luther King, Jr. New York: Random House, 1969.

Reviews the early and later stages of King's life and his struggle for economic and social freedom for blacks. Includes several photographs of King.

0207 *Faber, Doris, and Faber, Harold. The Assassination of Martin

Luther King, Jr. New York: Watts, 1978.

This work covers biographical information on King and studies the investigations surrounding his assassination.

0208 Flynn, James J. Negroes of Achievement in Modern America. New York: Dodd, Mead and Co., 1970.

Highlights the life and civil rights career of Dr. King.

0209 *Harris, Jacqueline L. Martin Luther King, Jr. New York: F. Watts, 1983.

The author traces the life of Dr. King and his use of nonviolence to bring about social change.

0210 *Harris, Janet and Hobson, Julius W. Black Pride; a People's Struggle by Janet Harris and Julius W. Hobson. New York: McGraw-Hill, 1969.

Gives information on King and his ability to establish equal rights for blacks in America.

0211 Hart, James D. The Oxford Companion to American Literature. New York: Oxford University Press, 1965, p. 445.

0212 Herzberg, Max J. The Reader's Encyclopedia of American Literature. New York: Thomas Y. Cromwell, Co., 1962, p. 571.

0213 Knight, Janet M., ed. Three Assassinations: The Deaths of John and Robert Kennedy and Martin Luther King. New York: Facts on File, pp. 1971-78.

Includes information on King's early childhood and his involvement with several protests and demonstrations during the civil rights movement.

0214 Kondrashov, S. The Life and Death of Martin Luther King. Moscow: Progress Publishers, 1981.

0215 Lichtenstein, Nelson, ed. Political Profiles: The Kennedy Years. New York: Facts on File, Inc., 1976, Vol. 3, pp. 286-289.

0216 Lichtenstein, Nelson, ed. Political Profiles: The Kennedy Years. New York: Facts on File, Inc., 1976, Vol. 4, pp. 334-339.

0217 Lomax, Louis E. To Kill a Black Man. California: Holloway House Pub., Co., 1968.

Gives a comparison of the lives of King and Malcolm X and their impact on society.

0218 Lewis, David L. King: A Critical Biography. Chicago: University of Illinois Press, 1978.

The life and times of King are discussed at length in this revised edition.

0219 Low, W. Augustus. Encyclopedia of Black America. New York: McGraw-Hill, 1981, pp. 486-589.

Digests the life and contributions of King during the civil rights movement.

0220 The McGraw-Hill Encyclopedia of World Biography. New York: McGraw-Hill, Inc., 1973, Vol. 6, pp. 204-207.

0221 Metcalf, George R. Black Profiles. New York: McGraw-Hill, 1970.

Gives an account of King's early life and educational training.

0222 *Miklowitz, Gloria D. Dr. Martin Luther King, Jr. New York: Tempo Books, 1977.

Contains a biographical sketch of King and his fight to end discrimination.

0223 *Millender, Dharathula H. Martin Luther King, Jr., Boy With a Dream. Indiana: Bobbs-Merrill, 1969.

Biography of Dr. King and his battle for equal rights.

0224 Miller, William Robert. Martin Luther King, Jr.: His Life, Martyrdom and Meaning for the World. New York: Weybright and Talley, Inc., 1968.

Accounts of King's early childhood, education and his development as a civil rights leader.

0225 Meritz, Charles, ed. Current Biography Yearbook: 1965. New York: H. W. Wilson Co., 1965.

Supersedes the biographical article that appeared in Current Biography 1957.

0226 Muller, Gerald Francis. Martin Luther King, Jr., Civil Rights Leader. Minnesota: T. S. Dennison & Co., 1971.

The early life of King while growing up in Atlanta is discussed in Chapter 1.

0227 Nasso, Christine, ed. Contemporary Authors: Permanent Series. Detroit, Michigan: Gate Research Co., 1978, Vol. 2, pp. 289-291.

Contains biographical information, as well as a listing of King's writings.

0228 Oates, Stephen B. Let the Trumpet Sound: The Life of Martin Luther King, Jr. New York: Harper & Row, Publishers, 1982.

This work is biographical in nature and covers a wide range of material on the slain civil rights leader.

0229 *Patterson, Lillie. Coretta Scott King. Champaign, Illinois: Garrard Publishing Co., 1977.

In this biographical account of Coretta, certain things are covered about Dr. King's personal life and his fight for justice.

0230 Preston, Edward. Martin Luther King: Fighter for Freedom. New York: Doubleday, 1968.

An overall look at King and his guest to eliminate racial segregation.

0231 Reddick, L. D. Crusader Without Violence: A Biography of Martin Luther King, Jr. New York: Harper & Brothers, Pub., 1959.

A biographical look at King and his ideology.

0232 Rush, Theressa G. Black American Writers Past and Present: A Bibliographical Dictionary. New Jersey: Scarecrow Press, Inc., 1975, Vol. 2, pp. 464-466.

0233 Schoenebaum, Eleanora, ed. Political Profiles: The Eisenhower Years. New York: Facts on File, Inc., 1977, Vol. 2, pp. 335-338.

0334 Searle, John D. Twentieth Century Christians. Edinburgh: Saint Andrews Press, 1977.

Chapter 9 sums up the life and times of Dr. King, including highlights of several demonstrations he was involved in.

0335 Spruill, Robert. Death & Life of Dr. Martin Luther King. New York: Carlton Pr., 1980.

0336 Steinberg, S. Seven Against Odds. New York: Vantage Press, Inc., 1981.

A brief biographical profile is given on Dr. King in Chapter 6.

0337 *Stevenson, Janet. Soldiers in the Civil Rights War; Adventures in Courage. Illinois: Reilly & Lee Books, 1971.

Includes biographical sketches of King and several other civil rights workers.

0338 Stuart, Karlton. Black History and Achievement in America. Arizona: Phoenix Bks., 1982.

A brief biographical sketch of Dr. King is mentioned in Chapter III.

0339 Time Inc. "I Have a Dream;" The Story of Martin Luther King in Text and Pictures. New York: Time Life Books, Inc., 1968.

0340 Fant, Clyde E. 20 Centuries of Great Preaching: An Encyclopedia of Preaching Vol. 12 Marshal to King. Waco, Texas: Word Books, 1971.

Gives biographical data on King and several of his sermons are discussed.

0341 Van Doren, Charles, ed. Webster's American Biographies. Massachusetts: G&C Merriam Co., 1974, p. 586.

0342 Vivian, Octavia. Coretta. Philadelphia: Fortress Press, 1970.

Events that took place in the life of Dr. King are mentioned in this biography of his wife.

0343 de Vries, Tjitte. Martin Luther King Marching On. Netherlands: Koninginneweg, 1968.

0344 Webb, Robert N. Leaders of Our Time. New York: Franklin Watts, Inc., 1965.

A biographical overview and King's involvement in the civil rights movement is given.

0345 Williams, John A. The King God Didn't Save. New York: Coward-McCann, Inc., 1970.

A study of King's life and how white power brought his life to an end.

0346 *Wilson, Beth P. Giants for Justice: Bethune, Randolph, and King. New York: Harcourt Brace Jovanovich, 1978.

The author gives a biographical outlook on King and his contributions to the civil rights movement.

0347 *Wilson, Beth P. Martin Luther King, Jr. New York: Putnam Pubs., 1971.

Covers the life and times of Dr. King and is primarily directed toward a juvenile audience.

0348 Wright, Elliot. Holy Company. New York: Macmillan, 1980.

A brief chronolog of King's involvement with the civil rights struggle is addressed.

0349 Yolen, Will. Heroes for Our Times. Harrisburg: Stackpole, Co., 1968.

Reflections of the life and ideology of Dr. King are discussed in Chapter 11.

ARTICLES

0350 "An Hour of Need." Time, Vol. 91, April 12, 1968, pp. 17-21.

A look at the life of Dr. King and the impact his death had on the nation.

0351 "Assassination Shocks Nation." Sr Schol, Vol. 92, April 25, 1968, pp. 1, 18-19.

Briefly recaptures the life and death of Dr. King.

0352 "Attack on the Conscience." Time, Vol. 69, February 18, 1957, pp. 17-20.

An overall look at King and what he has done for the civil rights movement.

0353 Baldwin, James. "The Dangerous Road Before Martin Luther King." Harper, Vol. 222, February, 1961, pp. 33-42.

A partial biography of King and his philosophical ideals are examined.

0354 Bennett, Lerone. "The Martyrdom of Martin Luther King." Ebony, Vol. 23, May 1968, pp. 174-181.

Examines the latter years of King leading up to his assassination.

0355 "Checklists of Change: The Civil Rights Drive: 1954-1968. Sr Schol, Vol. 93, September 20, 1968, pp. 8-9.

A brief background note is given on King and several other black leaders of the civil rights movement.

0356 Cleghorn, Reese. "Martin Luther King, Jr., Apostle of Crisis." Saturday Evening Post, Vol. 236, June 15, 1963, pp. 15-19.

A look at King and his influence in the civil rights movement and his fight for racial justice.

0357 Duggan, William R. "Three Men of Peace." Crisis, Vol. 81, December, 1974, pp. 331-334.

This article covers biographical information on King and two other civil rights leaders.

0358 "Even if I Die in the Struggle." US News World Rept, Vol. 64, April 15, 1968, p. 32.

An overview of King's life and his involvement with the civil rights struggle is discussed.

0359 Garland, Phyl. "'I've Been to the Mountaintop.'" Ebony, Vol. 23, May, 1968, pp. 124+.

An in-depth view of King and the events that transpired up until the time of his assassination.

0360 "Hero to Be Remembered." Ebony, Vol. 30, April, 1976, p. 134.

Highlights the life of King and the impact of his actions on blacks.

0361 "How Much Grief Can One Man Bear?" Ebony, Vol. 35, October, 1980, pp. 110-112+.

In his autobiography Daddy King reveals the impact of Martin's death on him and other family members.

0362 "King, from Montgomery to Memphis." Ebony, Vol. 25, April, 1970, pp. 172-174+.

A film that depicts the life of Dr. King is discussed.

0363 "King Is the Man, Oh Lord." Newsweek, Vol. 71, April 16, 1968, pp. 34-38.

Covers the life of Dr. King and discusses the impact of his death on the American society.

0364 "The Life and Death of Martin Luther King." Christ Today, Vol. 12, April 26, 1968, pp. 37-39.

Examines the life of King and his struggle for social justice.

0365 Long, Margaret. "Martin Luther King, Jr.: 'He Kept So Plan.'" Progressive, Vol. 32, May, 1968, pp. 20-24.

Accounts the life and times of King and his ability to keep his character in perspective throughout all the changes in his life.

0366 "Martin Luther King, Jr.: 1929-1968." Merch W, Vol. 100, April 8, 1969, p. 3.

0367 "Martin Luther King: Who He Is . . . What He Believes." US News World Rept, Vol. 58, April 5, 1965, p. 18.

A brief biographical sketch of Dr. King is given.

0368 "The Martyrdom of Martin Luther King, Jr." Crisis, Vol. 5, April, 1968, pp. 114-116.

Comments on the life of Dr. King and his significance in the civil rights movement. Episodes that followed the assassination of King are also given.

0369 "People." Time, Vol. 110, July 11, 1977, p. 45.

0370 "People of the Week." US News World Rept, Vol. 58, April 5, 1965, p. 18.

A brief biographical look at King is discussed along with his fight to eliminate segregation.

0371 Roeder, B. "Newsmakers." Newsweek, Vol. 90, July 11, 1977, p. 53.

A movie depicting the life of King is reviewed.

0372 Sitton, Claude. "King, Symbol of the Segregation Struggle." NY Times Mag, January 22, 1961, pp. 10+.

A biographical look at King and what he has done for the civil rights movement.

0373 "Ten Greats of Black History." Ebony, Vol. 27, August, 1972, p. 40.

A very brief view of King and what he accomplished in his fight against racial injustice.

0374 "Then Most Important Blacks in American History." Ebony, Vol. 30, August, 1975, p. 131.

Brief biographical sketch of King and his accomplishments.

0375 Thompson, E. B. "I've Been to the Mountaintop." Ebony, Vol. 23, May, 1968, pp. 124-136+.

A biographical overview of King in the civil rights movement up until the time of his death.

0376 "Transcendent Symbol." Time, Vol. 91, April 12, 1968, p. 19.

Discusses the early and late years of King and his involvement with the civil rights movement until his death.

0377 "A Tribute to Martin Luther King, Jr." Ebony, Vol. 20, December, 1964, pp. 126-127.

This article highlights the events of Dr. King's life and his accomplishments.

0378 Weisbrot, R. "Celebrating Dr. King's Birthday." New Repub, Vol. 190, January 30, 1984, pp. 10-12+.

A chronology of King's civil rights struggle is discussed.

GOVERNMENT DOCUMENTS

0379 U.S. Congress, House. Representative Yvonne Burke remarks on "Martin Luther King." 93rd Cong., 1st Sess., Cong Rec, Vol. 119, January 26, 1973, p. E2350.

Addresses the contributions of Dr. King to American society.

0380 U.S. Congress, House. Representative Charles B. Rangel speaking for "Honoring Dr. King." 97th Cong., 2nd Sess., Cong Rec, Vol. 128, June 10, 1982, pp. E2727-2728.

An article written about the contributions of King.

0381 U.S. Congress, Senate. Senator Yarborough remarks on "Tribute to Dr. Martin Luther King, Jr." 90th Cong. 2nd Sess., Cong Rec, Vol. 114, April 11, 1968, pp. S9696-9698.

The accomplishments of Dr. King's fight for civil rights are given.

0382 FBI Headquarters File. Memograph Dealing with Martin Luther King, Jr. March 11, 1968, Washington, D.C.: FBI Headquarters Murkin Security Files, 18 p. (Mem. No. 3526).

Contains an updated monograph on the life of King covering such areas as Communist affliations, proposed March on Washington, anti-Vietnam statements, an SCLC finances.

Southern Christian Leadership Conference

BOOKS

0383 Broderick, F. L. and Meier, A., eds. Negro Protest Thought in the Twentieth Century. Indianapolis: The Bobbs-Merrill, Co., 1965.

King has given his permission for the use of this reprint leaflet concerning the arms, purposes and philosophy of SCLC.

0384 Clayton, Edward, ed. The SCLC Story in Words and Pictures. Atlanta: The Southern Christian Leadership Conference, 1964.

King gives the aims and goals of SCLC's existence; includes a number of photographs of King and the members of SCLC involved in the civil rights movement.

0385 Ducas, G., ed. Great Documents in Black American History. New York: Praeger Pubs., 1970.

Includes references about SCLC's participation in the civil rights movement.

0386 Garrow, David J. Protest at Selma: Martin Luther King, Jr. and the Voting Rights Act of 1965. Connecticut: Yale University Press, 1978.

A study of the Southern Christian Leadership Conference and Dr. King and how their strategy influenced the passage of the Voting Rights Acts.

0387 Lewis, David L. King; A Critical Biography. Chicago: University of Illinois Press, 1978.

Outlines King's involvement with SCLC from its origin and the numerous civil rights demonstrations and campaigns.

0388 The McGraw-Hill Encyclopedia of World Biography. New York: McGraw-Hill, Inc., 1973, Vol. 6, p. 205.

An overview of SCLC and King's participation in this organization is given.

0389 Metcalf, George R. Black Profile. New York: McGraw-Hill, 1970.

Looks at the early development of SCLC and King's involvement with this organization throughout the civil rights movement.

0390 Mezu, S. Okeehukwu. Black Leaders of the Centuries. Buffalo, New York: Black Academy Pr., Inc., 1970.

Discusses King's involvement with SCLC and the civil rights movement.

0391 Oates, Stephen B. Let the Trumpet Sound: The Life of Martin Luther King, Jr. New York: Harper & Row, Publishers, 1982.

The author examines the operation and role of King and the SCLC.

0392 Stuart, Karlton. Black History and Achievement in America. Arizona: Phoenix Bks., 1982.

A brief history of SCLC and King's involvement with this organization is given.

ARTICLES

0393 "Abernathy's Army." Economist, Vol. 227, May 11, 1968, p. 22.

SCLC's Poor People's March on Washington begins with a memorial service for Dr. King in Memphis.

0394 Clark, Kenneth B. "The Civil Rights Movement: Momemtum and Organization." Dedalus, Vol. 95, Winter, 1966, pp. 239-267.

An historical look at black organizations throughout U.S. history; references are made about King and SCLC.

0395 Conconi, C. "Someone Had to Carry on for King." New Repub, Vol. 159, July 13, 1968, pp. 13-14.

Disarray plagues SCLC following the death of King. Dr. King's campaign of the Poor People's March on Washington lacks cohesiveness under Abernathy.

0396 Cotton, Dorothy. "A Conversation with Ralph Abernathy." J of the Current Soc Issues, Vol. 9, 1970, pp. 21-30.

Abernathy reveals his thoughts about SCLC and Dr. King.

0397 Doughs, C. C. "Ralph Abernathy, the Man Who Fights to Keep King's Dream Alive." Ebony, Vol. 25, January, 1970, pp. 40-42+.

Abernathy mentions the relationship between him and Dr. King and their work with the civil rights movement and SCLC.

0398 Fairclough, Adam. "The Southern Christian Leadership Conference and the Second Reconstruction, 1957-1973." South Atlantic Q, Vol. 80, Spring, 1981, pp. 177-194.

Fairclough covers an historical perspective of SCLC and Dr. King's involvement with this organization.

0399 Good, P. "No Man Can Fill Dr. King's Shoes, but Abernathy Tries." NY Times Mag, May 26, 1968, pp. 28-29+.

Compares the leadership ability of Dr. King and Abernathy and examines the organizational structure of SCLC since King's death.

0400 Goodman, G. "Doctor King, One Year After: He Lives, Man." Look, Vol. 33, April 15, 1969, pp. 29+.

Information about King becoming mentally and spiritually exhausted is revealed and some of the problems that developed in SCLC after the death of King.

0401 "The Keepers of the King Dream 15 Years Later." Ebony, Vol. 38, April, 1983, pp. 31-32+.

A look at several of King's close associates and their current status in American society.

0402 "The Men Behind Martin Luther King: SCLC Has Brilliant and Dedicated Staff." Ebony, Vol. 20, June, 1965, pp. 165-166+.

An inside look of SCLC and King's officers and staff members.

0403 "No Black Joshua." Economist, Vol. 228, August 24, 1968, p. 30.

Administrative changes are made in SCLC following the assassination of Martin Luther King.

0404 Osborne, J. "King's Men Return to Memphis." New Repub, Vol. 169, August 24, 1968, pp. 12-14.

Mentions the hotel where King was assassinated and the return of members of SCLC to Memphis for their annual convention.

0405 Randolph, A. Philip. "The 'March' - What Negroes Expected - What They Want Next." US News World Rept, Vol. 55, September 9, 1963, pp. 82-85.

King and SCLC are mentioned as one of the groups fighting for equality for blacks in America.

0406 Rogers, C. "Martin Luther King and Jesse Jackson: Leaders to Match Mountains." Christ Century, Vol. 89, January 12, 1972, pp. 29.

Looks at the appointment of Jesse Jackson by Dr. King as head of SCLC's Operation Breadbasket Program.

0407 Rogers, C. "SCLC: Rhetoric or Strategy?" Christ Century, Vol. 87, September2, 1970, p. 1032.

Comparisons of SCLC under Dr. King's leadership and the current leadership are made.

0408 Schardt, Arlie. "Tension, Not Split, in Negro Ranks." Christ Century, Vol. 82, May 12, 1965, pp. 614-616.

A comparison of King's SCLC organization and that of SNCC is given.

GOVERNMENT DOCUMENTS

0409 FBI Headquarters Files. Communist Prty, United States of America - Negro Question - SCLC. April 2, 1964, Washington, D.C.: FBI Headquarters Murkin Security Files, 7 p. (Int. Sec. No. 333)

An in-depth look at SCLC and King's involvement with the organization. Also, King gives certain financial disclosures about the organization.

0410 FBI Headquarters Files, Martin Luther King - Racial. June 10, 1963, Washington, D.C.: FBI Headquarters Murkin Security Files, 1 p. (Mem. No. 143).

Financial contributions to King and SCLC are revealed.

DISSERTATIONS AND THESES

0411 Morris, Aldon Douglas. "The Rise of the Civil Rights Movement and Its Movement: Black Power Structure 1953-1953." State University of New York at Stony Brook, DAI, 1980, 41:1241-A.

Dr. King's SCLC was listed as one of the major factors for the rise of the Civil Rights Movement.

0412 Walker, Eugene Pierce. "A History of the Southern Christian Leadership Conference, 1955-1965: The Evolution of a Southern Strategy for Social Change." Duke University, DAI, 1979, 40:2231-2232-A.

Attempts to clarify and bring about a better understanding of what Dr. King and SCLC were about.

Marches and Demonstrations

BOOKS

0413 Bishop, Jim. The Days of Martin Luther King, Jr. New York: G. P. Putnam's Sons, 1971.

Accounts are given of Dr. King and SCLC demonstrating in Albany, Georgia.

0414 Bishop, Jim. The Days of Martin Luther King, Jr. New York: G. P. Putnam's Sons, 1971.

Highlights of King and SCLC given on various civil rights campaigns.

0415 Congressional Quarterly Almanac. Washington, D.C.: Congressional Quarter Inc., 1975, Vol. 31, p. 523.

Looks at King's involvement with the voter registration protest in Selma.

0416 Congressional Quarterly Almanac. Washington, D.C.: Congressional Quarterly Inc., 1963, Vol. 19, p 374.

Mentions King's participation in the demonstration that was held in Washington.

0417 Congressional Quarterly Almanac. Washington, D.C.: Congressional Quarterly Inc., 1963, Vol. 19, pp. 336, 337.

Mentions the participation of King and SCLC in the activities of the Birmingham boycott.

0418 Cunningham, George J. Poor Black People. Michigan: Sherwood Forest Pubs., 1968.

Contains several photos of Dr. King and his civil rights activities.

0419 Davis, John P., ed. The American Negro Reference Book. Englewood Cliffs, N.J.: Prentice-Hall, 1966.

Chapter 11 highlights several demonstrations and marches that King was involved with.

0420 Dorman, Michael. We Shall Overcome. New York: Dial Press, 1964.

Chapter four discusses King's involvement in the Birmingham Demonstrations.

0421 Drimmer, Melvin, ed. Black History: A Reappraisal. New York: Doubleday & Company, Inc., 1968.

Examines the role of Dr. King in the Civil rights movement.

0422 Ducas, G., ed. Great Documents in Black American History. New York: Praeger Pubs., 1970.

An overview of the civil rights struggle is given with references to King as participant.

0423 Fager, Charles E. Selma, 1965. New York: Charles Scribner's Sons, 1974.

Covers the episodes and events that took place in Selma during the civil rights movement. Discusses King's presence and what role he played during this turbulent time.

0424 Not Used.

0425 Fishel, Leslie H. The Negro American: A Documentary History. Glenview, Ill.: Scott, Foresman and Co., 1967.

Chapter twelve discusses several of King's protest movements. An excerpt of his speech while in Washington is given.

0426 Franklin, John Hope and Meier, August. Black Leaders of the Twentieth Century. Illinois: University of Illinois Pr., 1982.

Chapter 13 focuses on King's involvement in the civil rights movement and his tactic of nonviolent demonstrations as a means to achieve equality for blacks.

0427 Garrow, David J. Protest at Selma: Martin Luther King, Jr. and the Voting Rights act of 1965. New Haven, Conn.: Yale University pr., 1978.

Chapter 4 includes events that took place at the Birmingham boycott and a statement from King outlining the goals of this campaign.

0428 Not Used.

0429 Gentile, Thomas. March on Washington: August 28, 1963. Washington, D.C.: New Day Publications, Inc. 1983.

0430 Grant, Joanne, ed. Black Protest: History Documents, an Analysis from 1619 to the Present. New York: Fawcett, 1968.

Examines several movement that King participated in during the civil rights period.

0431 Lawson, Steven F. Black Ballots: Voting Rights in the South, 1944-1969. New York: Columbia University Press, 1976.

Chapter 10 mentions the bombing of Dr. King's headquarters while leading protesters in Birmingham and several events that took place during the Selma campaign.

0432 Lyons, Thomas T. Black Leadership in American History. California: Addison-Wesley Pub. Co., 1971.

Several demonstrations and marches that were led by Dr. King are discussed in Chapter 5.

0433 Mars, Florence. Witness in Philadelphia. Baton Rouge: Louisiana State University Press, 1977.

Mars explores Dr. King's participation in a march that he led in Philadelphia, Miss.

0434 Martin Luther King, Jr.: The Journey of a Martyr. New York: Award Books, Universal Publishing and Distributing Corp., 1968.

A pictorial study of King and his personal episodes with the civil rights demonstrations. Various quotes from King on several issues concerning the civil rights movement are given.

0435 Metcalf, George R. Black Profile. New York: McGraw-Hill, 1970.

Numerous demonstrations and marches that were led by King are discuss.

0436 Mill, William Robert. Martin Luther King, Jr.: His Life, Martyrdom and Meaning for the World. New York: Weybright and Talley, Inc., 1968.

King and SCLC's various activities in the civil rights struggle are mentioned.

0437 Miller, William Robert. Martin Luther King, Jr.: His Life, Martyrdom and Meaning for the World. New York: Weybright and Talley, Inc., 1968.

The Birmingham boycotts, Chicago campaigns, March on Washington, and the Memphis strike are discussed.

0438 Muller, Gerald Francis. Martin Luther King, Jr., Civil Rights Leader. Minnesota: Denison, 1971.

Several chapters are devoted to demonstrations and marches that King was involved with during his civil rights career.

0439 Oates, Stephen B. Let the Trumpet Sound: The Life of Martin Luther King, Jr. New York: Harper & Row, Publishers, 1982.

The author examines some of the major demonstrations that King was involved in during his lifetime.

0440 Saunders, Doris, ed. The Day They Marched. Chicago: Johnson Publishing Co., 1963.

A commemoration of the March on Washington with photographs and a copy of King's "I Have a Dream" speech.

0441 Schlesinger, Arthur M., Jr. A Thousand Days: John F. Kennedy in the White House. Boston: Houghton Mifflin Co., 1965.

Observations are made concerning King and Kennedy encounters involving the Birmingham march and the March on Washington.

0442 Schulke, Flip, ed. Martin Luther King, Jr.: A Documentary, Montgomery to Memphis. New York: W. W. Norton & Inc., 197.

Contains a photographic view of King and his civil rights struggle.

0443 Sitkoff, Harvard. The Struggle for Black Equality, 1954-1980. New York: Hill and Wang, Inc., 1981.

The Montgomery bus boycott, boycott of Birmingham and the March on Washington are mentioned as major demonstrations that SCLC and Dr. King were involved with. Due to an error by the author, entry 0444 was eliminated.

0445 Steinberg, S. Seven Against Odds. New York: Vantage Press, Inc., 1981.

Chapter 6 covers several episodes of King's involvement with civil rights demonstrations, including Birmingham, Selma, and Memphis.

0446 Tweedle, John. A Lasting Impression; A Collection of Photographs of Martin Luther King, Jr. South Carolina: University of S.C. Pr., 1983.

Focuses on King's protest campaigns in Chicago.

0447 Webb, Robert N. Leaders of Our Time. New York: Franklin Watts, Inc., 1965.

Reviews several of King's mass demonstration attempts in Albany, Birmingham, and Jackson.

0448 Westin, Alan F. The Trial of Martin Luther King. New York: Crowell, 1974.

Studies the legal aspects of the marches and protests that Dr. King led in Birmingham.

0449 Wofford, Harris. Of Kennedys and Kings: Making Sense of the Sixties. New York: Farrar, Straus, Giroux, 1980.

Chapter two covers King's famous boycott and march to Montgomery and examines the circumstances surrounding the assassination of King.

ARTICLES

0450 "Acid Test; Swim - Integrators in St. Augustine." Newsweek, Vol. 63, June 29, 1964, pp. 26-27.

Reviews the events that took place between Dr. King and the business community during protest marches in that city.

0451 Adler, Renata. "Letter from Selma." New Yorker, Vol. 41, April 10, 1965, pp. 121-156.

A day-by-day account on the march from Selma to Montgomery. Several references are made about King and his participation in this event.

0452 "The Aimi Registration." Time, Vol. 85, January 29, 1965, pp. 20-21.

King arrives in Selma to aid in a voter's registration program for blacks.

0453 Barrett, George. "Jim Crow, He's Real Tired." NY Times Mag, March 3, 1957, pp. 1-74.

Observes Dr. King's struggle in Montgomery during the bus boycott and his fight throughout the South to end segregation.

0454 Barrett, George. "Montgomery: Testing Ground." NY Times Mag, December 16, 1956, pp. 8-9+.

Examines Montgomery after the bus boycott and the impact of King's tactics during the protest movement.

0455 Barrow, William. "Chicago Regrets." New Rep, Vol. 158, April 20,

1968, pp. 13-15.

Reflects on the relationship between Chicago and Dr. King during his fight for equality and fair housing.

0456 Bennett, L. "Biggest Protest March." Ebony, Vol. 19, November, 1963, pp. 29-31+.

Recaps the March on Washington and the effect of King's speech on the audience.

0457 "Birmingham Revisited." Time, Vol. 90, November 10, 1967, pp. 28-29.

King is jailed for demonstrating against segregated lunch counters and rest rooms.

0458 Booth, Richard. "The March of Time." Newsweek, Vol. 82, September 10, 1973, pp. 24-26.

Examines the March on Washington and what it accomplished a decade later. Several references are made about King and his impact during this march.

0459 "Bold Boycott Goes On." Life, Vol. 40, March 5, 1956, pp. 40-43.

Includes a picture of Dr. King after his arrest in Montgomery.

0460 Booker, Simeone. "50,000 March on Montgomery; Martin Luther King Leads Negroes, Whites in Most Heroic Civil Rights Protest in History." Ebony, Vol. 20, May, 1965, pp. 46-48+.

A pictorial view of the historical March on Montgomery is displayed.

0461 Bowles, Chester. "What Negroes Can Learn from Gandhi." Saturday Evening Post, Vol 230, March 1, 1958, pp. 19-21+.

Compares Dr. King's bus boycott with the struggles that Gandhi faced in South Africa.

0462 Braden, Anne. "Birmingham, 1956-1979: The History That We Made." South Expo, Vol. 7, N/A 1979, pp. 48-54.

Mentions King's participation in organizing protest marches in Birmingham.

0463 "Bus Boycott Leader Guilty." Sr Schol, Vol. 68, April 5, 1956, pp. 16-17.

Gives an account of King's arrest during the Montgomery bus boycott.

0464 "Camping-in for a Dream." Economist, Vol. 227, May 25, 1968, pp. 37-38.

The Poor People's March on Washington was a test to exercise the strength of SCLC leadership since the death of King.

0465 "The Central Point." Time, Vol. 85, March 19, 1965, pp. 23-28.

Covers the chaos in Alabama and Dr. King's call for a march from Selma to Montgomery.

0466 Chandler, R. "King in the Capital." Christ Today, Vol. 12, January 5, 1968, pp. 44-46.

Washingtonians and the religious community take a wait and see attitude about King's proposed March on Washington.

0467 "Civil Rights: Senate Buckles Down as Protests Build Up; Negro Leaders Push Demonstrations." Bus Week, May 9, 1964, pp. 26-27.

Dr. King and SCLC's plan for a state-wide boycott in Alabama is mentioned.

0468 Coburn, J. "Open City Chicago." New Repub, Vol. 155, September 17, 1966, pp. 9-10.

Comments on the failure of Dr. King's compromise on the fair-housing policy with city officials of Chicago.

0469 "Connor and King." Newsweek, Vol. 61, April 22, 1963, pp. 28+.

Details the arrest of King in Birmingham at a protest march.

0470 Cook, B. "King in Chicago." Commonweal, Vol. 84, April 29, 1966, pp. 175-177.

Dr. King explains his reasoning for shifting his protest movement to the North with special emphasis on Chicago.

0471 "Court vs King." Time, Vol. 89, June 23, 1967, p. 20.

The Supreme Court upholds the conviction of King for defying a court injunction against marching in Birmingham.

0472 "Day Martin Luther King Took Los Angeles." Sepia, Vol. 12, August, 1963, pp. 34-39.

0473 "Deacons Go North; Deacons for Defense and Justice Office in Chicago." Newsweek, Vol. 67, May 2, 1966, pp. 20-21.

King and SCLC's protest in Chicago is mentioned briefly.

0474 "Do or Die." Newsweek, Vol. 71, May 6, 1968, pp. 30-31.

The late Dr. King's Poor People's March on Washington is examined.

0475 "Doctor King Carries Fight to Northern Slums." Ebony, Vol. 21, April, 1966, pp. 94-102.

King takes his civil rights movement to Chicago to fight against the poor living conditions there.

0476 "Dr. King's Chicago Triumph." Crisis, Vol. 73, August-September, 1966, pp. 351-352.

The agreement reached between King and the city of Chicago can have an important impact on blacks' struggle for the right of residency.

0477 "Dogs, Kids, and Clubs." Time, Vol. 81, May 10, 1963, p. 19.

A description of the events that took place as King's marchers protested in the streets of Birmingham.

0478 Driscoll, Edward A. "Antitrespass Law Invoked." Christ Century, Vol 77, November 30, 1960, p. 1417.

King is arrested in Atlanta after participating in a sit-in against an all white lunch room.

0479 Dunbar, Ernest. "A visit with Martin Luther King." Look, Vol. 27, February 12, 1963, pp. 92-96.

Discusses the accomplishments of King in his civil rights struggle and what tasks lie ahead for the movement.

0480 "Electric Charge." Time, Vol. 85, March 26, 1965, pp. 19-20.

A look at Dr. King's planned march from Selma to Montgomery and the events that took place during this historic event.

0481 Fey, H. E. "Negro Ministers Arrested." Christ Century, Vol. 73, March 7, 1956, pp. 294-295.

Dr. King and twenty-three other black ministers are arrested for participating in the Montgomery boycott. Later he helps to calm an angry group of people outside his home after it was bombed.

0482 "Gamble in the Ghetto." Newsweek, Vol. 67, January 31, 1966, pp. 24-25.

A look at King's involvement with protests in Chicago about poor living conditions and segregated schools.

0483 "Georgia Justice." Nation, Vol. 191, November 5, 1960, pp. 338-339.

Studies the events that follow after King was fined for driving without a driver's license.

0484 "Go Slow, Dr. King!" Liberation, Vol. 8, June, 1963, p. 9.

Contains a statement from eight Alabama clergymen calling on King and the demonstrators to withdraw their demonstrations.

0485 Good, Paul. "Beyond the Bridge." _Reporter_, Vol. 32, April 8, 1965, pp. 23-26.

Examines the reasons that King and others decide to organize and carry out the march from Selma to Montgomery.

0486 Good, Paul. "Chicago Summer: Bossim, Racism, and Drinking." _Nation_, Vol. 203, September 19, 1966, p. 237-242.

King's proposed march on Cicero and his subsequent agreement on fair housing with Chicago is discussed.

0487 Griffin, John Howard. "Martin Luther King's Moment." _Sign_, Vol. 42, April, 1963, pp. 28-31+.

Contains an excerpt from the book _Thirteen for Christ_, which covers the story of the Montgomery Boycott and King's rise to prominence.

0488 Halberstam, David. "Second Coming of Martin Luther King." _Harper_, Vol. 235, August, 1967, pp. 39-51.

Dr. King directs his protest against the slums of the northern cities and the war in Vietnam.

0489 "Hard Choice Ahead for the Movement: King's Nonviolent Civil Rights Approach." _Bus Week_, April 13, 1968, pp. 30-32.

Raises questions about the future of the civil rights movement following the death of Dr. King.

0490 Harper, Gene. "Holding Fast to the Dream." _Soldiers_, Vol. 39, January, 1984, pp. 18-29.

Includes photos and a description of the 20th anniversary of the 1963 March on Washington.

0491 Hentoff, Nat. "A Peaceful Army." _Commonweal_, Vol. 72, June 10, 1960, pp. 275-278.

A closer look at the civil rights movement and the role that Dr. King plays in this ongoing situation.

0492 Hepburn, Dave. "'Rat Pack' Give $50,000 to Reverend Martin Luther King." _Sepia_, Vol. 9, April, 1961, pp. 42-47.

Mentions Dr. King and several other leaders as being one of the reasons which brought them back to Washington.

0493 Hooks, B. L. "Twentieth Anniversary Mobilization: Jobs, Peace and Freedom." _Crisis_, Vol. 90, October, 1983, pp. 22-23.

Mentions Dr. King and several other leaders as being one of the reasons which brought them back to Washington.

0494 "It Looks Like a 'Hot Summer' - With Selma the Beginning." _US_

News World Rept, Vol. 58, March 22, 196, pp. 32-33.

Looks at King's involvement in protest marches and his plea for better participation from white clergymen.

0495 Johnson, Walter. "Historians Join the March on Montgomery." South Atlantic Q, Vol. 79, Spring, pp. 158-174.

American historians observe the final day of King's historic march from Selma to Montgomery.

0496 Kempton, M. "March on Washington." New Repub, Vol. 149, September 14, 1963, pp. 19-20.

Mentions King's role as a participant in the march.

0497 "King Comes to Chicago." Christ Century, Vol. 82, August 11, 1964. pp. 979-980.

Discusses King's participation in several demonstrations against the superintendent of public schools.

0498 "King's Targets." Newsweek, Vol. 63, June 22, 1964, pp. 26+.

A look at the protest in Tuscaloosa and the events leading up to the arrest of Dr. King.

0499 Kopkind, A. "Selma." New Repub, Vol. 152, March 20, 1965, pp. 7-9.

Alludes to several problems King encountered while preparing to march from Selma to Montgomery.

0500 "Life and Death of Martin Luther King." Sepia, Vol. 17, June, 1968, pp. 9-22.

Covers the civil rights activities of King while protesting in Memphis and the funeral ceremony of the slain civil rights leader.

0501 "Long Live the King." Newsweek, Vol. 47, April 2, 1956, p. 26.

Dr. King is convicted for leading the bus boycott in Montgomery.

0502 "Man of Peace Leads -- a Second March That Ends in a Prayer." Life, Vol. 58, March 19, 1965, pp. 32-34.

Covers photographs of clergymen kneeling in prayer during the Selma to Montgomery march.

0503 "Man Who Was a Fool." Sepia, Vol. 6, February, 1962, pp. 31-33.

0504 "March to Montgomery." Sr Schol, Vol. 86, April 1, 1965, pp. 8-10.

Examines the march that King led on Route 80 protesting voting rights for blacks in Alabama.

0505 "Marching Where?" Reporter, Vol. 35, July 14, 1966, pp. 12+.

Comments are made concerning the dissension between King and the members of SNCC and CORE while demonstrating in Mississippi.

0506 "March's Meaning; March on Washington." Time, Vol. 82, September 6, 1963, pp. 13-15.

King and other leaders express their optimism about the march. This article also includes excerpts of King's "I Have a Dream" speech.

0507 "Martin Luther King's Georgia Battleground." Sepia, Vol. 11, October, 1962, pp. 36-39.

0508 "Memphis: An Ugly New Portent." Newsweek, Vol. 71, April 8, 1968, pp. 33-34.

Examines the impact of King's presence in Memphis during the sanitation strike.

0509 "Memphis Blues." Time, Vol. 91, April 5, 1968, p. 25.

Reviews the violence and looting that ensued while King was leading a protest march in Memphis.

0510 Miller, Perry. "The Mind and Faith of Martin Luther King." Reporter, Vol. 19, October 30, 1958, p. 40.

Gives an account of the bus boycott in Montgomery.

0511 "Montgomery Boycott." Nation, Vol. 182, February 11, 1956, p. 102.

King is constantly harassed by the police and eventually is jailed for speeding.

0512 "No Peace for Winner of Peace Prize." US News World Rept, Vol 58, February 1, 1965, p. 19.

King launches a massive voter registration drive in Selma.

0513 "Notes and Comments." New Yorker, Vol. 59, September 12, 1983, pp. 37-38.

An analysis of the twentieth anniversary of King's March on Washington is given.

0514 "Now Dr. King's Marchers Turn North." US News World Rept, Vol. 58, May 3, 1965, p. 8.

King leads demonstrators in Boston to protest against unfair practices in housing and public schools.

0515 Oates, Stephen B. "The Week the World Watched Selma." Am Herit, Vol. 33, June/July, 1982, pp. 48-63.

Covers the march led by King from Selma to Montgomery and its impact on voting rights legislation.

0516 "On to Montgomery." Newsweek, Vol. 65, March 29, 1965, pp. 21-22.

King receives legal clearance to carry out his march from Selma to Montgomery and is assured by the authorities that violence would be constrained in future marches.

0517 Oudes, Bruce J. "The Siege of Cicero." Nation, Vol. 204, March 27, 1967, pp. 398-401.

A look at the city of Cicero and Dr. King's proposed threat to march there.

0518 "Peace with Justice." Commonweal, Vol. 78, May 31, 1963, p. 268.

King comments on remarks made by Birmingham religious leaders regarding blacks demonstrating.

0519 Peters, W. "Man Who Fights Hate With Love." Redbook, Vol. 117, September, 1961, pp. 36-37+.

Looks at the struggles and adversities that King faced in his fight for civil rights.

0520 "Poorly Timed Protest." Time, Vol. 81, April 19, 1963, pp. 30-31.

Demonstrators are led by King in Birmingham to protest against unfair hiring practices and segregated lunch counters.

0521 "Powerful New Movie; King -- From Montgomery to Memphis." Ebony, Vol. 25, April, 1970, pp. 173-174+.

Critiques a film based on the factual aspects of King's involvement with marches and demonstrations throughout the U.S.

0522 "Prophetic Ministry?" Newsweek, Vol. 60, August 20, 1962, pp. 78-79.

Studies King's involvement in the Civil rights movement, with special emphasis on the Albany movement.

0523 Rivers, C. K. "The Day King Marched in Chicago." Negro Digest, Vol. 15, March, 1966, pp. 54-58.

King addresses the social problems of the city, especially the battle between the black community and the schools' superintendent.

0524 Rudman, Norman G. "Who Loves a Parade: Walker v. City of Birmingham." Law in Transition Q, Vol. 9, December, 1967, pp. 185-219.

Examines the Supreme Court decision to uphold the criminal convictions of Dr. King and others for demonstrating in Birmingham.

0525 Satter, David O. "West Side Story." New Repub, Vol. 155, July 2, 1966, p. 15-19.

Dr. King's fight for housing improvement in Chicago is mentioned.

0526 Schreiber, N. "A Last Tribute." Pop Photogr, Vol 91, February, 1984, p. 34.

Photos of Dr. King while he campaigned in Chicago are discussed.

0527 Schulz, W. "Martin Luther King's March on Washington." Read Digest, Vol. 92, April, 1968, pp. 65-69.

Examines the prospects of a major crisis for the U.S. government with Dr. King's planned March on Washington.

0528 "The Selma Campaign." Natl Rev, Vol. 17, March 23, 1965, pp. 227-28.

Through his nonviolent methods Dr. King was able to defeat the local authorities.

0529 "Shades of Bull Connor." Newsweek, Vol. 65, February 1, 1965, pp. 21-22.

Examines the confrontation between King and Sheriff Clark during a demonstration in Selma.

0530 "The Siege of Selma." Nation, Vol. 200, February 15, 1965, pp. 154-55.

Discusses the tactics that King and his organization used when they prepared for civil rights marches.

0531 Stevenson, Janet. "Rosa Parks Wouldn't Budge." Am Herit, Vol. 23, February, 1972, pp. 56-65+.

A look at the events that led to the Montgomery bus boycott and King's organizational plans to initiate this protest.

0532 "Summer Strategy." Newsweek, Vol. 65, April 12, 1965, pp. 28-29.

A discussion of King's plan for an economic boycott of Alabama and a voter registration drive covering several states in the South.

0533 "Swift Deliverance." Time, Vol. 76, November 7, 1960, p. 30.

King is arrested in Atlanta then released the very next day.

0534 Talese, Gay. "Where's the Spirit of Selma Now? NY Times Mag, May 30, 1965, pp 8-9+.

Brief comments on the effect Dr. King had on the people of Alabama are mentioned and changes that were brought about in Selma because of the march.

0535 Thornton, J. Mills, III. "Challenge and Response in the Montgomery Bus Boycott of 1955-56." Alabama Rev, Vol. 33, July, 1980, pp. 163-235.

A look at the events leading to the bus boycott and arguments as to whether the real demands of the boycott were really met.

0536 Thrasher, T. R. "Alabama's Bus Boycott." Reporter, Vol. 14, March 8, 1956, pp. 13-16.

Interprets the boycott as a question as to whether human rights should be granted to everyone in the human race.

0537 "Tough Years Ahead." Newsweek, Vol. 66, August 30, 1965, pp. 19-20.

Looks at Dr. King's visit to Watts after the riot.

0538 "Truce in Chicago: Freedom March Cracks the Ghetto's Limits." Bus Week, Vol. 5, September 3, 1966, pp. 36-38.

Dr. King and SCLC come to an agreement with the city of Chicago on the issues of open housing and residential integration.

0539 "Victory in Jail." Time, Vol. 85, February 12, 1965, pp. 16-17.

Dr. King succeeds with his plan to register black voters in Selma.

0540 "Violence Versus Nonviolence." Negro Hist Bull, Vol. 24, April, 1961, pp. 147+.

Discusses King's arrest and sentencing at a sit-in in Atlanta and the events that took place afterwards.

0541 Wainwright, Loudon. "Martyr of the Sit-Ins." Negro Hist Bull, Vol. 24, April, 1961, pp. 147-51+.

Covers the arrest and conviction of King in Georgia for protesting in a segregated restaurant.

0542 "Dr. Martin Luther King Gets New Woe, Prestige." Life, Vol. 49, November 7, 1960, pp. 123-124+.

0543 "Waiting for Miracles." Time, Vol. 80, August 3, 1962, pp. 12-13.

Studies the difficulties King faced while demonstrating in Albany, Georgia for racial justice.

0544 Walton, Norman W. "Waking City, a History of the Montgomery Boycott." Negro Hist Bull, Vol. 20, October-November, 1956, pp. 16-20+.

An account of the factors and events leading to the Montgomery boycott. Several references are made to King and his involvement in this movement.

0545 "We Have Got to Deliver Nonviolent Results." Newsweek, Vol. 68, August 22, 1966, pp. 58-59.

A discussion of several demonstrations by King and his followers and violent attacks by whites because of the demonstrations.

0546 "When Dr. King Went to Jail Again." US News World Rept, Vol. 53, July 23, 1962, p. 10.

A look at the implications surrounding Dr. King's arrest in Albany, Georgia.

0547 "When the 'Freedom March' Hits Washington." US News World Rept, Vol. 55, August 12, 1963, pp. 26-27.

Defines what the March on Washington is all about and what Dr. King hopes to accomplish.

0548 "Where Racial Trouble Keeps Erupting; St. Augustine, Fla." US News World Rept, Vol. 57, July 6, 1964, p. 6.

King requests federal help to combat the violence between white and black demonstrators.

0549 Worsnop, Richard L. "Mass Demonstrations." Edit Res Rep, Vol. 2, August 14, 1963, pp. 585-602.

A look at various civil rights demonstrations with references from King on the success and failure of several campaigns.

GOVERNMENT DOCUMENTS

0550 U.S. Congress, House. Representative C. Albert commenting on "The K's and Law and Order." 88th Cong., 1st Sess., Cong Rec, Vol. 109, May 15, 1963, pp. H8613-8614.

Contends that the reason for trouble and bloodshed in Birmingham was caused by Dr. King stirring up racial hatred.

0551 U.S. Congress, House. Representative George W. Andrews comments on "Our Visiting Clergy and Selma." 89th Cong., 1st Sess., Cong Rec, Vol. 111, March 29, 1965, pp. H6263-6264.

King and other demonstrators are accused of agitating violence and racial disharmony in Selma.

0552 U.S. Congress, House. Representative John M. Ashbrook commenting on "Reappraisal of Civil Disobedience and Nonviolence Policies Needed." 90th Cong., 2nd Sess., Cong Rec, Vol. 114, April 23, 1963, pp. H10392-10393.

Contends that King was largely responsible for his own demise and advises his followers to discontinue the scheduled protests around the country.

0553 U.S. Congress, House. Representative Edward I. Derwinski remarks on "Invasion of Washington by Martin Luther King." 90th Cong., 2nd Sess., Cong Rec, Vol. 114, January 22, 1968, RE574.

King's proposed March on Washington could lessen congressional legislation for blacks.

0554 U.S. Congress, House. Representative Devine remarks on "Payment for Costs of Demonstrations." 90th Cong., 2nd Sess., Cong Rec, Vol. 114, April 3, 1968, p. H8775.

Contends that legislation should be enacted that would require King to post a bond before he can carry out any demonstrations.

0555 U.S. Congress, House. Representative W. Dickinson on "March on Montgomery - The Untold Story." 89th Cong. 1st Sess., Cong Rec, Vol. 111, March 30, 1965, pp. H6333-6335

Reveals that a number of King's followers were Communist and that he was quite aware of it.

0556 U.S. Congress, House. Representative D. Edwards and Buchanan comments on "King's Proposed Boycott." 98th Cong., 1st Sess., Cong Rec, Vol. 111, April 1, 1965, pp. H6768-6769.

Expresses shock over reports that King has decided to initiate a boycott in Mobile.

0557 U.S. Congress, House. Representative E. Gathings remarks on "Dr. Martin Luther King." 89th Cong., 1st Sess., Cong Rec, Vol. 111, March 29, 1965, p. H6264.

Comments on King's proposed demands for the boycott in Alabama.

0558 U.S. Congress, House. Representative K. Hechler speaking against "Alabama Boycott Is Nonsense." 89th Cong., 1st Sess., Cong Rec, Vol. 111, April 1, 1965, pp. H6746-6747.

Feels that King's call for withdrawal of federal funds from Alabama would have a devastating impact on the nation's space program in Alabama.

0559 U.S. Congress, House. Representative H. Kornegay comments on "The President's Personal Sacrifice for Peace in the World Suggests That Dr. King Can Do No Less Here at Home." 90th Cong., 2nd Sess., Cong Rec, Vol. 114, April 3, 1968, p. H8822.

Due to the violence in Memphis while King was there, several Congressmen suggest that he should call off his planned March on Washington.

0560 U.S. Congress, House. Representative D. Kuykendall and Everett remarks on "Memphis Agitation Created by Martin Luther King." 90th Cong., 2nd Sess., Cong Rec, Vol. 114, April 1, 1968, pp. H8380-8381.

Reactions to King's involvement in Memphis are given.

0561 U.S. Congress, House. Representative James Martin remarks on "Catholic Paper Calls for Return to Reason in Alabama Situation." 89th Cong., 1st Sess., Cong Rec, Vol. 111, April 1, 1965, pp. A1600-1601.

An editorial suggests that King and other civil rights leaders discontinue with their marches and demonstrations and concentrate on more pressing needs for blacks.

0562 U.S. Congress, House. Representative James Martin remarks on "King's Boycott Immoral." 89th Cong., 1st Sess., Cong Rec, Vol. 111, April 12, 1965, pp. A1767-1768.

Concludes that King's proposed boycott would prove to be a social and economic mistake.

0563 U.S. Congress, House. Representative James Martin comments on "Martin Luther King Would Hurt Negroes in Drive for Power." 89th Cong., 1st Sess., Cong Rec, Vol. 111, April 12, 1965, pp. A1780-1781.

Maintains that King had personal motives for the boycott in Alabama and very little concern for the citizens of that state.

0564 U.S. Congress, House. Representative Martin remarks "On Boycotting Alabama." 89th Cong., 1st Sess., Cong Rec, Vol. 111, April 5, 1965, p. H6876.

Believes that the Vice President is in agreement with King's proposed boycott of Alabama.

0565 U.S. Congress, House. Representative C. Mize remarks on "Economic Boycott of Alabama Will Harm Civil Rights Cause." 89th Cong., 1st Sess., Cong Rec, Vol. 111, March 29, 1965, p. H6267.

Believes that a voter registration bill can be worked out in Congress provided that King calls for an end of demonstrations in Alabama.

0566 U.S. Congress, House. Representative J. Pickle speaking for "The Riot Prevention and Control Act of 1967." 1967, pp. H20563-20564.

Inserts a statement by Dr. King and other leaders calling for an end to rioting and looting in the cities.

0567 U.S. Congress, House. Representative John R. Rarick remarks on "Ven cere mos: We Shall Overcome." 90th Cong., 2nd Sess., Cong Rec, Vol. 114, April 23, 1968, pp. E10395-10401.

Mentions King as one of the reasons for the demonstrations and violence in America.

0568 U.S. Congress, House. Representative R. Roberts commenting on "Demonstrations in Birmingham." 88th Cong., 1st Sess., Cong Rec,

Vol. 109, May 15, 1963, pp. H8600-8601.

Refers to a telegram asking Dr. King to call an end to the boycott in Birmingham.

0569 U.S. Congress, House. Representative B. Rogers comments on "Proposed Intimidation an Insult to the Congress." 90th Cong., 1st Sess., Cong Rec, Vol. 113, October 24, 1967, pp. H29822-29823.

States that Dr. King's proposed demonstrations to pressure Congress on the passage of certain legislation should be considered an insult to that legislative body.

0570 U.S. Congress, House. Representative W. Ryan remarks on "Danger in Albany." 87th Cong., 1st Sess., Cong Rec, Vol. 108, August 1, 1962, pp. H15320-15321.

Addresses the situation that King and other civil rights groups faced while protesting in Albany.

0571 U.S. Congress, House. Representative A. Selden speaking against "Disruption of Peace and Order in our Nation's Capital." 90th Cong., 2nd Sess., Cong Rec, Vol. 114, January 17, 1968, p. 130.

Seeks an injunction against King in order to prevent his planned demonstrations in Washington.

0572 U.S. Congress, House. Representative A. Seldon remarks on "Dr. Martin Luther King's Plans for Activity in Washington in April." 90th Cong., 2nd Sess., Cong Rec, Vol. 114, February 7, 1968, p. H2435.

Contains a letter sent to the U.S. Attorney General informing him of planned activities by King and his organization in Washington.

0573 U.S. Congress, House. Representative R. Sikes speaking against "Unneeded Racial Problems." 88th Cong., 1st Sess., Cong Rec, Vol. 109, May 13, 1963, p. H8361.

Contends that King's civil rights actions in Birmingham were a disgrace to the people of America.

0574 U.S. Congress, House. Representative John M. Slack, Jr. remarks on "Who Can Think of a Better Way." 89th Cong., 1st Sess., Cong Rec, Vol. 111, February 9, 1965, p. A538.

Feels that King's protests and demonstrations were wrong, but so were the voting registration requirements in Alabama.

0575 U.S. Congress, House. Representative J. Waggoner commenting on "Race Relations." 88th Cong., 1st Sess., Cong Rec, Vol. 109, May 16, 1963, pp. H8783-8784.

Dr. King and several of his associates are accused of being professional racists and instrumental in arousing local disorder in Birmingham.

0576 U.S. Congress, Senate. Senator W. Byrd comments on "April 15 Anti-Vietnam Demonstrations." 90th Cong., 1st Sess., Cong Rec, Vol. 113, April 14, 1967, p. S9702.

Dr. King is announced as the principal speaker in the New York protest rally against the war in Vietnam.

0577 U.S. Congress, Senate. Senator W. Byrd speaking against "Memphis Riots and the Coming March on Washington." 90th Cong., 2nd Sess., Cong Rec, Vol. 114, March 29, 1968, pp. S8263-8266.

Contends that Washington can expect the same events by King and his followers that took place in Memphis.

0578 U.S. Congress, Senate. Senator W. Byrd comments on The Memphis Riot and the Proposed March on Washington." 90th Cong., 2nd Sess., Cong Rec, Vol. 114, April 4, 1968, p. S8946.

Calls for an injunction of King's planned march on the capital; also contains statements from King regarding the injunction and his reaction to it.

0579 U.S. Congress, Senate. Senator W. Byrd comments on "The Spring Campaign of Martin Luther King." 90th Cong., 2nd Sess., Cong Rec, Vol. 114, February 7, 1968, pp. S2495-2496.

Contends that King's proposed march would cause several problems for his followers and government officials.

0580 U.S. Congress, Senate. Senators F. Clark and J. Javits speaking against "Jailing of Dr. Martin Luther King." 87th Cong., 2nd Sess., Cong Rec, Vol. 108, July 11, 1962, pp. S13275-13276.

Feels that the arrest of King was unwise and unjust, and that the state of Georgia was in violation of the 14th Amendment.

0581 U.S. Congress, Senate. Senator S. Holland comments on "Interference With Civil Rights." 90th Cong., 2nd Sess., Cong Rec, Vol. 114, February 5, 1968, pp. S2094-2099.

King's proposed March on Washington and the building of the shanty town will not bring equality for blacks in the area of jobs and income overnight.

0582 U.S. Congress, Senate. Senator H. Humphrey speaking for "A Bill to Eliminate Discrimination in Interstate Commerce." 85th Cong., 1st Sess., Cong Rec, Vol. 103, January 9, 1957, p. 5367.

Mentions that an Alabama police officer conspired to kill Dr. King.

0583 U.S. Congress, Senate. Senator J. Javits speaking against "Imprisonment of Martin Luther King in St. Augustine, Fla." 88th Cong., 2nd Sess., Cong Rec, Vol. 110, June 13, 1964, pp. S13690-13691.

Calls for the release of King from jail on charges of trespassing.

0584 U.S. Congress, Senate. Senator G. Smathers remarks on "Time for a Think-in." 89th Cong., 1st Sess., Cong Rec, Vol. 111, April 5, 1965, pp. S6924-6925.

King's protest actions in the past and his boycott in Alabama typifies disrespect for law and order.

0585 U.S. Congress, Senate. Senator J. Stennis comments on "King's Arrest." 88th Cong., 2nd Sess., Cong Rec, Vol. 110, June 12, 1964, pp. 51642-13643.

Remarks on King's demonstrations and protests in St. Augustine, Florida.

0586 U.S. Congress, Senate. Senator S. Thurmond commenting on "Are Racial Riots Communist Inspired?" 88th Cong., 1st Sess., Cong Rec, Vol. 109, August 2, 1963, pp. S13968-13975.

Several references are made about King's Communist associates and the effect they had on his decision to stage demonstrations.

0587 U.S. Congress, Senate. Senator S. Thurmond commenting on "Washington Post Article on Bayard Rustin, Leader of March on Washington." 88th Cong., 1st Sess, Cong Rec, Vol. 109, August 13, 1963, pp. S14836-14839.

Directs criticism at King for his involvement with Rustin and his Communist activities.

0588 FBI Headquarters Files. Boycott of Alabama by the Southern Christian Leadership Conference Protesting Voter Discrimination. April 5, 1965, Washington, D.C.: FBI Headquarters Murkin Security Files, 3 p. (Encl. No. 1221).

Examines the material of a news conference that King has called to outline his reasons for an economic boycott of Alabama.

0589 FBI Headquarters Files. A Brief Summary of the Current Situation at Selma and Marion, Alabama.

Observes the movement and activity of King in Selma after he announces an intensive voter registration drive.

0590 FBI Headquarters Files. Martin Luther King and Associates in Mississippi. July 23, 1964, Washington, D.C.: FBI Headquarters Murkin Security Files, 4 p. (Mem No. 404).

Agents keep a close watch on King and give an outline of his intinerary while in Mississippi.

0591 FBI Headquarters Files. Martin Luther King, Jr. April 20, 1962, Washington, D.C.: FBI Headquarters Murkin Security Files, 2 p. (Sec. Mat. No. 48).

An informant reveals that King and several others are organizing a civil rights society.

0592 FBI Headquarters Files. Martin Luther King, Jr. Security Matter, July 9, 1965, Washington, D.C.: FBI Headquarters Murkin Security Files, 3 p. (Encl. No. 1694).

Agents reveal information regarding King's agenda while staying in Los Angeles.

0593 FBI Headquarters Files. Martin Luther King Sponsors Voter Registration Demonstrations in Alabama. February 19, 1965, Washington, D.C.: FBI Headquarters Murkin Security Files, 2 p. (Encl. No. 893).

Looks at King's involvement at a mass rally in Wilcox County protesting against voting irregularities.

0594 FBI Headquarters Files. Martin Luther King - Violence in Memphis. April 1, 1968, Washington, D.C.: FBI Headquarters Murkin Security Files, 4 p. (Encl. No. 3291).

Reveals that King was distraught as a result of the violence that occurred in Memphis and considered not returning to that city and calling off the March on Washington.

0595 FBI Headquarters Files. Racial Situation - Albany, Georgia Racial Matters. July 24, 1962, Washington, D.C.: FBI Headquarters Murkin Security Files, 5 p. (Mem. No. 84).

A summary of King's involvement in the Albany demonstrations is given.

0596 FBI Headquarters Files. Sanitation Workers Strike, Memphis, Tenn. April 1, 1968, Washington, D.C.: FBI Headquarters Murkin Security Files, 3 p. (Tel. No. 3273).

Members of King's organization outline their protest plans for the city of Memphis.

0597 FBI Headquarters Files. Washington Spring Project. February 20, 1968, Washington, D.C.: FBI Headquarters Murkin Security Files, 10 p. (End. No. 3227).

Contains an outline of King and SCLC's reasons for their proposed Poor People's March.

0598 FBI Headquarters Files. Washington Spring Project, March 20, 1968, Washington, D.C.: FBI Headquarters Murkin Security Files, 4 p. (Tel. No. 3249).

King visits several cities in Mississippi seeking volunteers to join him and SCLC on their protest March on Washington.

DISSERTATIONS & THESES

0599 Coleman, Susie Helen. "Martin Luther King's Chicago Campaign: An Experiment in Paradox." Master's Thesis, Austin Peay State University, 1969.

Examines the differences of nationwide support for marches in the South and the North.

0600 Gillman, Thomas J. "The Montgomery Bus Boycott of 1955-1956." Master's Thesis, Auburn University, 1968.

An in-depth study of the boycott and the role that SCLC and Dr. King played in this historical event.

0601 Millner, Steven Michael. "The Montgomery Bus Boycott: Case Study in the Emergence and Career of a Social Movement." University of California, Berkeley, DAI, 1981, 42:3315-A.

An in-depth look at this boycott and how King emerged as the leader of this movement.

0602 Yeakey, Lamont H. "The Montgomery, Alabama Bus Boycott, 1955-56." Columbia University, DAI, 1979, 41:776-A.

Mentions Dr. King as being one of the new black leaders emerging from the boycott and SCLC as an organization to be reckoned with in the movement.

Major Awards

BOOKS

0603 Bishop, Jim. The Days of Martin Luther King, Jr. New York: G. P. Putnam's Sons, 1971.

Reactions to King's acceptance of the Nobel Peace Prize and general responses by the public are discussed.

0604 Bishop, Jim. The Days of Martin Luther King, Jr. New York: G. P. Putnam's Sons, 1971.

King is awarded the Spingarn Medal for his contribution to race relations.

0605 Curtis, C. J. Contemporary Protesant Thought. New York: Bruce Pubs. Co., 1970.

Includes an excerpt of an acceptance speech by King after receiving the Noble Peace Prize.

0606 Knight, Janet M., ed. Three Assassinations: The Death of John and Robert Kennedy and Martin Luther King. New York: Facts on File, Inc., 1971. Vol. 1.

King is awarded the Nobel Peace Prize for his involvement with nonviolent demonstrations.

0607 Knight, Janet M., ed. Three Assassinations: The Death of John and Robert Kennedy and Martin Luther King. New York: Facts on File, Inc., 1971.

Details a number of awards and memorials honoring the late Dr. King.

0608 Lewis, David L. King; A Critical Biography. Chicago, University of Illinois Press, 1978.

The events and activities of King are mentioned following his nomination for the Nobel Peace Prize.

0609 Miller, William Robert. Martin Luther King, Jr.: His Life, Martyrdom and Meaning for the World. New York: Weybright and Talley, Inc., 1968.

Mentions several awards that King received for his fight and involvement in the civil rights movement.

ARTICLES

0610 "A Remarkable Dinner and . . . Off to Jail." Life, Vol. 58, February 12, 1965, pp. 34-34A.

King is honored by whites and blacks in Atlanta because he was a recipient of the Nobel Peace Prize. He continues his civil rights protest by returning to Selma for a voter registration drive.

0611 "Atlanta Rose to the Occasion." Christ Century, Vol. 82, February 10, 1965, p. 164.

A tribute is paid to King by the black and white community for his winning the Nobel Peace Prize.

0612 "Doctor King's Nobel Prize." America, Vol. 111, October 31, 1964, p. 503.

Tribute is paid to Dr. King for receiving the Nobel Peace Prize and his other accomplishments involving civil rights.

0613 "Dr. Martin Luther King's Never Ending Crusade for Peaceful Non-Violent Integration Paid Off With Nobel Peace Prize." Sepia, Vol. 13, December, 1964, p. 38.

0614 "Endorse Dr. King for Nobel Prize." Christ Century, Vol. 81, August 12, 1964, p. 1006.

Reasons are given as to why King should be awarded the Nobel Peace Prize.

0615 "How Martin Luther King Won the Nobel Peace Prize." US New World Rept, Vol. 58, February 8, 1965, pp. 76-77.

An in-depth look at why and how King was awarded the Nobel Peace Prize.

0616 "King Proposed for Peace Prize." Christ Century, Vol. 81, February 12, 1964, p. 198.

Several members of the Swedish government nominate King for the Nobel Peace Prize.

0617 "King Receives Nobel Prize." Christ Century, Vol. 81, October 28,

1964, p. 1324.

King comments after receiving the news that he would receive the Nobel Peace Prize.

0618 "Man of Conflict Wins a Peace Prize." US News World Rept, Vol. 57, October 26, 1964, p. 24.

Discussion of King's winning the Nobel Peace Prize and the support he received as a recipient.

0619 "Man of the Year." Nation, Vol. 198, January 13, 1964, pp. 41-42.

Explores some underlying facts as to why Time magazine chose to make Dr. King Man of the Year.

0620 "Martin Luther King, Jr. Man of 1963." Negro Hist Bull, Vol. 27, March, 1964, pp. 136-137.

King is named Man of the Year by Time magazine; chronologs the events that took place in his life during that year.

0621 "Nobleman King." Newsweek, Vol. 64, October 26, 1964, p. 77.

Discusses King's reaction when he hears that he will be awarded the Nobel Peace Prize.

0622 Padley, Robert B. and Archer, F. M. "Nobel Prize for King?" Christ Century, Vol. 81, October 21, 1964, p. 1308.

Applauds the suggestion that King be awarded the Nobel Peace Prize.

0623 "Peace Medal; Awarded St. Francis Peace Medal." Cath Mess, Vol. 81, October 17, 1963, p. 12.

0624 "Peace Prize Causes Controversy." Christ Century, Vol. 82, January 13, 1965, p. 39.

Looks at the possibility of a problem developing in Atlanta over the proposed banquet for King.

0625 "Rare Tribute." Time, Vol. 85, February 5, 1965, p. 24.

Whites in Atlanta honor King for winning the Nobel Peace Prize.

0626 Sanders, Charles L. "The Torturous Road to Oslo." Ebony, Vol. 20, March, 1965, pp. 36+.

Discussion of King's acceptance of the Nobel Peace Prize, and the events that took place while he traveled through Europe.

0627 "The Saturday Review - Anisfiled-Wolf Awards." Saturday Rev, Vol. 12, May 30, 1959, p. 12.

King is presented this award for writing the book Stride Toward

Freedom.

0628 "Splendid Victory for the 'Concerned.'" Life, Vol. 58, February 12, 1965, p. 4.

Reviews some of the problems that came about when it was announced that the city of Atlanta would honor Dr. King for winning the Nobel Peace Prize.

0629 "Two Good Choices." Nation, Vol. 199, November 9, 1964, p. 319.

King, along with Satre, are elected to receive the Nobel Peace Prize.

0630 "Up from Montgomery." Newsweek, Vol. 64, December 21, 1964, pp. 40-41.

King accepts the Nobel Peace Prize and discusses his philosophy of nonviolence.

0631 "The Youngest Ever." Time, Vol. 84, October 23, 1964, p. 27.

Reactions to King's being named the recipient of the Nobel Peace Prize.

0632 "The Youngest Ever." World Affairs, Vol. 30, November, 1964, p. 20.

GOVERNMENT DOCUMENTS

0633 FBI Headquarters Files. Acceptance of Nobel Peace Prize. October 16, 1964, Washington, D.C.: FBI Headquarters Murkin Security Files, 3 p. (Encl. No. 491).

King tries to decide what he should do with the prize money that he receives for winning the Nobel Peace Prize.

0634 FBI Headquarters Files. King Receives Freedom Award. April 29, 1965, Washington, D.C.: FBI Headquarters Murkin Security Files, 1 p. (Airtel No. 1287).

Mentions King's acceptance of the Pacem in Terris Peace and Freedom Award from the Davenport Catholic Interracial Council.

0635 FBI Headquarters Files. Nobel Peace Prize. November 12, 1964, Washington, D.C.: FBI Headquarters Murkin Security Files, 4 p. (Encl. No. 521).

Details the plans of a celebration for Dr. King upon his receiving the Nobel Peace Prize.

FBI and Government Operations

BOOKS

0636 Bishop, Jim. The Days of Martin Luther King, Jr. New York: G. P. Putnam's Sons, 197.

Chapters I and IV mention the FBI's ongoing activities against King by tapping his phone.

0637 Congressional Quarterly Almanac. Washington, D.C.: Congressional Quarterly Inc., 1964, Vol. 20, p. 379.

King and Hoover agree to meet and iron out their differences.

0638 Congressional Quarterly Almanac. Washington, D.C.: Congressional Quarterly Inc., 1975, Vol. 31, pp. 387, 408-412.

Reveals the activities of the FBI's campaign to discredit King by bugging, blackmail and intimidation.

0639 Garrow, D. J. The FBI and Martin Luther King, Jr.: From "Solo" to Memphis, New York: W. W. Norton & Co., 1981.

Studies the FBI's investigation into SCLC ad King on various civil rights activities.

0640 Knight, Janet M., ed. Three Assassinations: The Death of John and Robert Kennedy and Martin Luther King. New York: Facts on File, Inc., 1978, Vol. 2.

An extensive study of the FBI's campaign to discredit King as a public figure is disclosed. Also reveals the Hoover-King controversy.

0641 Oates, Stephen B. Let the Trumpet Sound: The Life of Martin Luther King, Jr. New York: Harper & Row, Publishers, 1982.

Several references are made to the FBI and their activities against Martin Luther King.

0642 Scott, Peter Dale. The Assassinations: Dallas and Beyond - A Guide to Cover-ups and Investigations. New York: Vintage Books, 1976.

Includes excerpts of the following in regard to King's assassination: 1) questions relating to a conspiracy by Harold Weisberg, 2) and in-depth interview with James Earl Ray by Wayne Chastain and 3) a reprinting of Hoover's Cointelepro documents against King.

0643 Sitkoff, Harvard. The Struggle for Black Equality, 1954-1980. New York: Hill and Wang, Inc., 1981.

Chapter 6 looks at the personal dislike by President Johnson and Hoover of King and the methods they used to try and discredit him.

0644 Whitehead, Don. Attack on Terror: The FBI Against the Ku Klux Klan in Mississippi. New York: Funk and Wagnalls, 1970.

Includes statements made by Dr. King about the FBI's lack of concern for the safety of the civil rights workers.

ARTICLES

0645 Burnham, M. A. "If King Could See Us Now." Freedomways, Vol. 22, First Quarter, 1982, pp. 3-12.

Discusses the attempts of the FBI to discredit King as a fraudulent civil rights leader and studies the opinions of King that are still being voiced today.

0646 "Crusade to Topple King." Time, Vol. 106, December 1, 1975, pp. 11-12.

Insights into how and why Hoover was so obsessed with discrediting King.

0647 "Dispute Between Hoover and King." US News World Rept, Vol. 57, December 7, 1964, p. 46+.

Hoover remarks about certain statements King made concerning the role of the FBI in civil rights matters.

0648 "The FBI and Civil Rights: J. Edgar Hoover Speaks Out." US News World Rept, Vol. 57, November 30, 1964, pp. 56-58.

Hoover discusses his attitude toward Dr. King and the civil rights movement.

0649 Hogan, L. D. "Is There a Nobel Prize for Peephole Journalism?" Commonweal, Vol. 110, December 16, 1983, pp. 687-689.

Compares the smear tactics of the Polish government on Lech Walensa to that of Dr. King and the FBI operations.

0650 Hoover, J. Edgar. "The FBI and Civil Rights - J. Edgar Hoover Speaks Out." US News World Rept, Vol. 57, November 30, 1964, pp. 56-58.

Attacks the character of King, and Dr. King gives his reaction to the statements made against him.

0651 "Hoover-King Hassle." Sepia, Vol. 14, January, 1965, pp. 74-75.

0652 "The Hoover-King Meeting." Newsweek, Vol. 69, December 14, 1964, pp. 22+.

King meets with Hoover to discuss problems he felt could be corrected with the FBI in the Southern region.

0653 "Knives Sharpening." Natl Rev, Vol. 16, December 15, 1964, p. 1094.

Mentions the function of the FBI and Hoover's attack on Dr. King's character.

0654 Navasky, Victor S. "The Government and Martin Luther King." Atlantic, Vol. 226, November, 1970, pp. 43-52.

Explores the confusion surrounding the tapping of King's telephone by the government.

0655 "Off Hoover's Chest." Newsweek, Vol. 64, November 30, 1964, pp. 29-36.

Criticizes King's statement about the inability of the FBI in the Southern offices.

0656 Rowan, C. T. "Is There a Conspiracy Against Black Leaders?" Ebony, Vol. 31, January 1976, pp. 39-40.

Studies the parties involved who tried to discredit King and oust him from power in the civil rights movement.

0657 Salmans, S. and Marro, A. "Tales of the FBI." Newsweek, Vol. 86, December 1, 1975, pp. 35-36.

A Senate committee reveals information involving the FBI and their activities of hate campaigns against Dr. King

0658 Scott, P. "Martin Luther King, Jr. and the Tapes." Am Opinion, Vol. 21, December, 1978, pp. 11-13+.

Calls on Congress to make an examination of FBI tapes that were gathered on Dr. King.

GOVERNMENT DOCUMENTS

0659 U.S. Congress, Senate. Select Committee to Study Governmental Operations with Respect to Intelligence Activities. Intelligence Activities. Senate Resolution 21, V.6: Federal Bureau of Investigation. 94th Cong., 1st Sess., Washington, D.C.: Congressional Information Service, Inc., 1976, (CIS No. 76-S961-6).

This report reveals the reasons for the FBI investigation of Dr. King and reviews the techniques used to discredit King and other individuals.

0660 U.S. Congress, Senate. Select Committee to Study Governmental Operations with Respect to Intelligence Activities. Supplementary Detailed Staff Reports on Intelligence Activities and the Rights of Americans, Book 3. 94th Cong., 2nd Sess., Washington, D.C.: CIS, Inc., 1976, (CIS No. 7-S963-3).

Results on governmental operations involving the civil liberties of King and others.

0661 U.S. Congress, House. Subcommittee on Civil and Constitutional Rights. FBI Oversight, Part 3. 94th Cong., 1st Sess., Washington, D.C.: CIS, Inc., 1976, (CIS No. 77-H521-9.9).

Reviews FBI operations that tried to discredit Dr. King and examines ways to prevent any reoccurrences.

0662 U.S. Congress, House. Representative John Bryant remarks on "Smear." 98th Cong., 1st Sess., Cong Rec, Vol. 129, October 19, 1983, pp. E4983-4984.

Comments on demonstrations held in an attempt to discredit King and includes an article that discusses the FBI's activities against the slain civil rights leader.

0663 U.S. Congress, House. Representative R. Garcia remarks on "The FBI's War on Martin Luther King." 98th Cong., 1st Sess., Cong Rec, Vol. 129, July 18, 1983, p. E3541.

Comments on the FBI's abuse of power involving the rights of Dr. King.

0664 U.S. Congress, House. Representative N. Smith remarks on "The Facts About Martin Luther King, Jr." 98th Cong., 1st Sess., Cong Rec, Vol. 129, November 7, 1983, pp. H9296-9298.

Addresses testimonies by Hoover regarding his reasons for wire tapping Dr. King's phone.

0665 FBI Headquarters Files. Article by Jack Anderson and Les Whitten Concerning Martin Luther King, Jr. October 20, 1975, Washington, D.C.: FBI Headquarters Murkin Security Files, 8 p. (Mem. No. 3966).

The Bureau responds to allegations that they tried to discredit King by leaking information about his alleged Communist affiliations and his personal sex life.

0666 FBI Headquarters Files. Approval of Wiretaps and Microphones by R. F. Kennedy - Specific Approval of Wiretaps on Martin Luther King. May 21, 1968, Washington, D.C.: FBI Headquarters Murkin Security Files, 2 p. (Mem. No. 3457).

Explores the possibility of a FBI report dealing with King's sex life being leaked to the public.

0667 FBI Headquarters Files. Approval of Wiretaps and Microphones by Robert F. Kennedy. May 28, 1968, Washington, D.C.: FBI Headquarters Murkin Security Files, 2 p. (Mem. No. 3472).

Information regarding Kennedy's authorizing the FBI's wiretap on King's telephone is discussed.

0668 FBI Headquarters Files. Cassius M. Clay, Jr. June 9, 1969, Washington, D.C.: FBI Headquarters Murkin Security Files, 2 p. (Mem. No. 3595).

Questions are raised as to whether the wiretaps on King's phone were authorized by the Attorney General and for how long.

0669 FBI Headquarters Files. Edgar Hoover. April 15, 1968, Washington, D.C.: FBI Headquarters Murkin Security Files, 2 p. (Corr. No. 3317).

Hoover denies making a statement about King being financed by Communists.

0670 FBI Headquarters Files. Editor of the Evening Star Calls. June 19, 1969, Washington, D.C.: FBI Headquarters Murkin Security Files, 5 p. (Mem. No. 3638).

The FBI answers allegations involving illegal wiretaps of Dr. King's phone and seeks to clarify Robert Kennedy's involvement in the situation.

0571 FBI Headquarters Files. Information Concerning Martin Luther King., Jr. April 20, 1962, Washington, D.C.: FBI Headquarters Murkin Security Files, 2 p. (Letter No. 45).

Hoover relays information to the White House about King and his involvement in organizing a civil rights society.

0672 FBI Headquarters Files. J. Edgar Hoover. April 16, 1968, Washington, D.C.: FBI Headquarters Murkin Security Files, 2 p. (Corr. No. 3316).

Hoover admits calling King a liar, but denies that he ever denounced him as a Communist.

0673 FBI Headquarters Files. Martin Luther King Appointment with

Director. December 2, 1964, Washington, D.C.: FBI Headquarters Murkin Security Files, 10 p. (Mem. No. 634).

Discusses the results of an in-depth meeting between King and Hoover in an attempt to reconcile their differences on the FBI's protection for civil rights marchers.

0674 FBI Headquarters Files. Martin Luther King, Jr. June 18, 1969, Washington, D.C.: FBI Headquarters Murkin Security Files, 1 p. (Mem. No. 3602).

Facts concerning a telephone wiretap of King's home are revealed.

0675 FBI Headquarters Files. Martin Luther King, Jr. August 20, 1970, Washington, D.C.: FBI Headquarters Murkin Security Files, 1 p. (Mem. No. 3795).

Response to a letter received by the FBI denying allegations that the Bureau blackmailed Dr. King is given.

0676 FBI Headquarters Files. Martin Luther King, Jr. August 26, 1970, Washington, D.C.: FBI Headquarters Murkin Security Files, 1 p. (Mem. No. 3822).

Additional information regarding Hoover's use of a wiretap to monitor King's personal life is given.

0677 FBI Headquarters Files. Martin Luther King, Jr. December 18, 1975, Washington, D.C.: FBI Headquarters Murkin Security Files, 3 p. (Corr. No. 4070).

A concerned group demands that the President, FBI, and Attorney General apologize to Mrs. King for their illegal operations against Dr. King.

0678 FBI Headquarters Files. Martin Luther King, Jr. - Allegations of a Former Special Agent. May 25, 1973, Washington, D.C.: FBI Headquarters Murkin Security Files, 2 p. (Mem. No. 3949).

Allegations are raised concerning the FBI's attempt to persuade community leaders not to attend a banquet honoring Dr. King in Atlanta.

0679 FBI Headquarters Files. Martin Luther King, Jr.: Attacks on the Director as a Result of an Erroneous Article. August 18, 1970, Washington, D.C.: FBI Headquarters Murkin Security Files, 2 p. (End. No. 3834).

Monitors the events and reactions of the public following the publication of an article that dealt with wiretapping operations by Hoover on Dr. King.

0680 FBI Headquarters Files. Martin Luther King Meets with Hoover. December 2, 1964, Washington, D.C.: FBI Headquarters Murkin Security Files, 4 p. (Encl. No. 607).

Hoover submits a letter to the President discussing in detail the meeting that was held between him and King.

0681 FBI Headquarters Files. Martin Luther King, Jr. - Security Matters. August 7, 1973, Washington, D.C.: FBI Headquarters Murkin Security Files, 2 p. (Mem. No. 3951).

A former FBI agent reveals some of the wrong doings of the Bureau in connection with Dr. King.

0682 FBI Headquarters Files. Martin Luther King, Jr. Security Matter - Communist. November 19, 1964, Washington, D.C.: FBI Headquarters Murkin Security Files, 3 p. (Mem. No. 537).

Details the rough draft of a speech written for King on the subject of Hoover's criticism of King's integrity.

0683 FBI Headquarters Files. Martin Luther King Plans to Accept an Award. February 1, 1965, Washington, D.C.: FBI Headquarters Murkin Security Files, 2 p. (Mem. No. 799).

Information regarding the possibility of King being given an award by a Catholic organization is revealed. The Bureau hopes to disrupt this type of activity in the near future.

0684 FBI Headquarters Files. Ramsey Clark, Television Appearance on David Frost Program. August 6, 1969, Washington, D.C.: FBI Headquarters Murkin Security Files, 2 p. (Mem. No. 3664).

Attorney General Clark answers questions regarding the FBI's abuse of power in regard to Dr. King.

0685 FBI Headquarters Files. Telegram from Martin Luther King, Jr. Dated November 19, 1964 Civil Rights Matters. November 20, 1964, Washington, D.C.: FBI Headquarters Murkin Security Files, 4 p. (Mem. No. 581).

Remarks by Hoover regarding statements King made about the FBI.

Philosophy

BOOKS

0686 Adler, Bill, ed. The Wisdom of Martin Luther King, in His Own Words. New York: Lancer books, 1968.

An overview of the ideology of King on such subjects as non-violence, love and hate, brotherhood, and the search for world peace.

0687 Ansbro, John J. Martin Luther King, Jr.: The Making of a Mind. New York: Orbis Books, 1982.

An in-depth analyses of men that influenced King's thinking on civil disobedience and nonviolence.

0688 Bates, James D. The Martin Luther King Story: A Study in Apostasy, Agitation and Anarchy. Tulsa, Oklahoma: Christian Crusade Publications, 1967.

Bales presents information to the reader so that he can decide whether King was an enemy of America and a Communist.

0689 Bedau, Hugo Adam, ed. Civil Disobedience: Theory and Practice. New York: Pegasus, 1969.

King's "Letter from Birmingham Jail" is give, along with arguments about his theory of civil disobedience.

0690 Berry, Mary Frances and John W. Blassingame. Long Memory: The Black Experience in America. New York: Oxford University Pr., 1982.

0691 Bishop, Jim. The Days of Martin Luther King, Jr. New York: G. P. Putnam's Sons, 1971.

Chapter IV discusses King's anti-war stance on Vietnam.

0692 Bishop, Jim. The Days of Martin Luther King, Jr. New York:

G. P. Putnam's Sons, 1971.

Several chapters interpret King's ideology of nonviolence as a tool to secure social justice for blacks in America.

0693 Bosmajian, Haig A., and Bosmajian, Hamida, comps. The Rhetoric of the Civil Rights Movement. New York: Random House, 1969.

A copy of Dr. King's famous "Letter from Birmingham City Jail" is discussed by the authors.

0694 Carmichael, Stokely. Stokely Speaks: Black Power Back to Pan-Africanism. New York: Random House, 1971.

0695 Cartwright, John H., ed. Essays in Honor of Martin Luther King, Jr. Illinois: Leiffer Bureau of Social and Religious Research, 1971.

Critiques several of King's social, political, economic, and theological beliefs and the impact of his philosophy on our society.

0696 Castagna, Edwin. Caught in the Act. New Jersey: Scarecrow Press, 1982.

King's philosophy of nonviolence was strongly influenced by the writings and teachings of Gandhi.

0697 Civil Disobedience; Five Essays. Public Affairs Conference Center, Ohio, 1968.

Storing examines and criticizes King's philosophy of nonviolent resistance.

0698 Clark, Kenneth B. The Negro Protest: James Baldwin, Malcolm X, Martin Luther King Talk with Kenneth B. Clark. Boston: Beacon Press, 1963.

0699 Clayton, Edward, ed. The SCLC Story in Words and Pictures. Atlanta: The Southern Christian Leadership Conference, 1964.

An interpretation of King's "Letter from a Birmingham Jail" is given.

0700 Cleage, Albert B., Jr. Black Christian Nationalism: New Direction for the Black Church. New York: William Morrow and Co., 1972.

References are made in Chapter 7 to the content of King's "I Have a Dream" speech.

0701 Cleage, Albert B., Jr. The Black Messiah. New York: Sheed and Ward, 1968.

Chapter 15 discusses the affect that King had on mobilizing blacks in America and creating confrontations between whites and blacks.

0702 Cone, James H. Black Theology and Black Power. New York: Seabury Press, 1969.

Examines King's theological philosophy and its relationship with the black power movement.

0703 Curtis, C. J. Contemporary Protestant Thought. New York: Bruce Pubs., Co., 1970.

A definition of King's theological philosophy is given; his feelings concerning the theory of nonviolence is discussed in Chapter 13.

0704 Davis, John P., ed. The American Negro Reference Book. Englewood Cliffs, N.J.: Prentice-Hall, 1966.

Chapter 10 analyzes the philosophy of non-violence as practiced by Dr. King.

0705 "Dear Dr. King . . ." A Tribute in Words and Pictures by Children of the Richard J. Bailey School. Jamaica, New York: Buckingham Enterprises, Inc., 1968.

Chapter Two contains an extensive study of King's Nobel Peace Prize acceptance speech.

0706 Duberman, M. B. The Uncompleted Past. New York: Random House, Inc., 1965.

A review of Dr. King's book Where Do We Go From Here is discussed.

0707 Edmund, T. Martin Luther King and the Black Americans' Protest Movement in the U.S.A. Delhi: Rainbow Book Co., 1976.

An analysis of King's philosophy and the affect of his leadership on the black protest movement is examined.

0708 Goodwin, Bennie E. Reflections on Education. Meditations on King, Friere and Jesus as Social and Religious Educators. East Orange, N.J.: Goodpatrick Pub., 1978.

In Chapter Two Goodwin attempts to explain how King's philosophy brought about a social change in America.

0709 Hamilton, Charles V. The Black Preacher in America. New York: William Morrow and Co., 1972.

Reveals King's preaching style and theological teachings regarding political and social action.

0710 Harcourt, Melville, ed. Thirteen for Christ. New York: Sheed and Ward, Inc., 1963.

Chapter 2 mentions Dr. King as one of the men that demonstrated the true teachings of Christ.

Play for Martin Luther King. Alabama: Religious Education Pr., 1969.

Ideological differences between King and Malcolm X are presented in this play, along with excerpts of King's "I Have a Dream" speech.

0712 Jones, Major J. Black Awareness: A Theology of Hope. Nashville: Abingdon Press, 1971.

Chapters 6 and 7 examine King's philosophy of nonviolence and his theological beliefs.

0713 King, Coretta. My Life With Martin Luther King, Jr. New York: Holt, Rinehart, and Winston, 1969.

0714 Lewis, Anthony. Portrait of a Decade: The Second American Revolution. New York: Random House, 1964.

A look at Dr. King's practice of nonviolent action, along with several of his key civil rights demonstrations.

0715 Lincoln, C. Eric. Martin Luther King, Jr.: A Profile. New York: Hill and Wang, 1970.

Interpretations by several authors of some of King's most noteworthy undertakings in the civil rights movement.

0716 Lincoln, C. Eric., ed. Is Anybody Listening to Black America? New York: Seabury Press, 1968.

Chapters One and Two reveal several of King's ideologies along with analyses from other authors.

0717 Lokos, Lionel. House Divided: The Life and Legacy of Martin Luther King. New Rochelle, NY: Arlington House, 1968.

Lokos feels that Dr. King left his country and people a legacy of lawlessness, not peace.

0718 Lynd, S., ed. Nonviolence in America: A Documentary History. Indianapolis: The Bobbs-Merrill Co., Inc., 1966.

Addresses the ideology of King on such subjects as: civil disobedience, nonviolence and love.

0719 Lyons, Thomas T. Black Leadership in American History. California: Addison-Wesley Pub. Co., 1971.

Analyzes King's response to the growth of the black power ideology in America.

0720 Lyons, Thomas T. Black Leadership in American History. California: Addison-Wesley Pub. Co., 1971.

Covers activities and statements made by King during his

In Chapter 5 statements made by King during his anti-Vietnam War campaign are discussed.

0721 Lyons, Thomas T. Black Leadership in American History. California: Addison-Wesley Pub. Co., 1971.

Pages 191-194 explore the historical development of King's philosophy of nonviolence.

0722 Metcalf, George R. Black Profiles. New York: McGraw-Hill, 1970.

Discusses the philosophical development of Dr. King.

0723 Mezu, S. Okechukwu. Black Leaders of the Centuries. Buffalo, New York: Black Academy Press, Inc., 1970.

Explores the ideas and philosophies of Dr. King.

0724 Miller, Elizabeth W. The Negro in America: A Bibliography. Cambridge, Mass.,: Harvard University Press, 1970.

A brief listing of works written by and about King.

0725 Miller, William Robert. Martin Luther King, Jr.: His Life, Martyrdom and Meaning for the World. New York: Weybright and Talley, Inc., 1968.

Contains an analysis of King's "I Have a Dream" speech along with several other references to his philosophy on various subjects.

0726 Moses, Wilson J. Blacks, Messiahs, and Uncle Toms: Social and Literary Manipulations of Religious Myth. University Park, PA: Penn State University Press, 1982.

0727 Paris, Peter J. Black Leaders in Conflict: Joseph H. Jackson, Martin Luther King, Jr., Malcolm X, Adam Clayton Powell, Jr. New York: Pilgrim Pr., 1978.

Discusses the differences between King's and other black leaders approaches to civil rights matters.

0728 Reavis, Ralph. Martin Luther -- Martin Luther King, Jr. and the Black Experience. Quantico, Va: Flame International, 1982.

Compares the philosophies of Martin Luther and Dr. King in regard to social consciousness.

0729 Romero, Patricia W., ed. In Black America: 1968, the Year of Awakening. Washington, D.C.: United Publishing Corp., 1969.

0730 Rose, T., ed. Violence in America. New York: Random House, 1969.

Eldridge Cleaver discusses the impact of King's death on the American public, and the effect of King's philosophy of nonviolence on the civil rights movements.

0731 Schuchter, Arnold. White Power/Black Freedom Planning the Future of Urban America. Boston: Beacon Press, 1968.

The views of Dr. King are compared to those of Malcolm X.

0732 Scott, Robert L., and Brockriede, Wayne. The Rhetoric of Black Power. New York: Harper and Row, Publishers, 1969.

Dr. King expresses his views on black power, while others interpret King's ideology on the same subject.

0733 Scruggs, Julius R. Baptist Preachers with Social Consciousness: A Comparative Study of Martin Luther King, Jr. and Harry Emerson Fosdick. Penn.: Dorrance & Co., 979.

Scruggs attempts to compare the ideology and events that shaped the philosophy of King and Fosdick on the subject of social awareness.

0734 Searle, John D. Twentieth Century Christians. Edinburgh: Saint Andrews Press, 1977.

The "I Have a Dream" speech is summarized in Chapter 9.

0735 Sharp, Gene. The Politics of Nonviolent Action. Boston: Porter Sargent Pub., 1973.

Brief observations on some of King's ideology concerning the civil rights movement.

0736 Sitkoff, Harvard. The Struggle for Black Equality, 1954-1980. New York: Hill and Wang, Inc., 1981.

Chapter 7 mentions Dr. King's anti-war statements concerning the United States' involvement in Vietnam.

0737 Smith, Arthur L. Rhetoric of Black Revolution. Boston: Allyn and Bacon, Inc., 1969.

Discusses King's philosophy and his style of speaking to the audience.

0738 Smith, Ervin. The Ethics of Martin Luther King, Jr. New York: Edwin Mellen Pr., 1982.

0739 Smith, Kenneth and Zepp, Ira G. Search for the Beloved Community: The Thinking of Martin Luther King, Jr. Valley Forge, Pa: Judson Press, 1974.

Attempts to give an historical viewpoint of King's theological and philosophical development.

0740 Stang, Alan. It's Very Simple -- The True Story of Civil Rights. Belmont: Western Islands Pub., 1965.

Contends that Dr. King and other top civil rights leaders were either Communists or controlled by Communists.

0741 Steinberg, S. Seven Against Odds. New York: Vantage Press, Inc., 1981.

Chapter 6 stresses a key point on racial pride among blacks in King's Nobel Peace Prize acceptance speech.

0742 Walton, Hanes Jr. The Political Philosophy of Martin Luther King, Jr. Connecticut: Greenwood Press, 1971.

Describes the substance of King's political philosophy and its early beginnings and demonstrates King's ability to put his philosophy in practice.

0743 Wilmore, Gayrand S. Black Religion and Black Radicalism. Garden City, New York: Doubleday & Co., 1972.

0744 Young, Henry J. Major Black Religious Leaders Since Nineteen-Forty. Nashville, TN: Abingdon, 1979.

Reviews the influences on King's way of thinking and analyzes several of his theological and sociological concepts.

ARTICLES

0745 Abernathy, R. "My Last Letter to Martin." Ebony, Vol. 23, July, 1968, pp. 58-61.

Recollections of his work with Dr. King in the civil rights movement from the very beginning up until King was assassinated.

0746 Auer, Bernhard M. "A Letter from the Publisher." Time, Vol. 85, March 19, 1965, p. 21.

Explains the reasons for selecting Dr. King as a subject for the front cover of their magazine.

0747 Banks, S. L. "Dr. Martin Luther King, Jr., Remembered: The Fractured Dream." J Negro Hist, Vol. 67, Fall, 1982, pp. 195-197.

Contends that King's hope for an equal share in the socioeconomic wealth of America has not changed, and in some cases has even worsened.

0748 Bennett, Lerone, Jr. "The South and the Negro." Ebony, Vol. 12, April, 1967, pp. 77+.

Several issues dealing with civil rights and racial harmony are addressed by King.

0749 Bosmajian, H. "Inaccuracies in the Reprintings of Martin Luther King's "I Have a Dream" Speech. Comm Educ, Vol. 31, April, 1982, pp. 107-114.

0750 Bosmajian, Haig A. "The Rhetoric of Martin Luther King's 'Letter from a Birmingham Jail.'" Midwest Q, Vol. 21, Autumn 1979, pp. 46-62.

Analyzes the form and technique that King used to reach Americans in his appeal for equal rights.

0751 Bosmajian, Haig A. "The Rhetoric of Martin Luther King's 'Letter from a Birmingham Jail.'" Midwest Q, Vol. 8, January, 1967, pp. 127-143.

0752 Brody, J. "Measure of King." Nation, Vol. 222, April 10, 1976, pp. 420-421.

Assesses the principles of King and the effect they had on blacks.

0753 Capeci, Dominic J., Jr. "From Harlem to Montgomery: The Bus Boycott and Leadership of Adam Clayton Powell, Jr. and Martin Luther King, Jr." Historian, Vol. 41, August, 1979, pp. 721-237.

The sociological, psychological, and ideological developments of King and Powell are compared.

0754 Carter, George E. "Martin Luther King: Incipient Transcendentalist." Phylon, Vol. 40, December, 1979, pp. 318-324.

Discusses Thoreau as an important figure in developing certain aspects of King's philosophy.

0755 Carter, Jimmy. "Accepting the Martin Luther King, Jr. Nonviolent Peace Prize." W Comp Pres Docs, Vol. 15, January 22, 1979, pp. 27-33.

Comments on King's basic philosophy and his accomplishments in the civil rights struggle.

0756 Colaiaco, James A. and Adam Fairclough. "Martin Luther King, Jr. and Movement for Social Change." Phylon, Vol. 45, March, 1984, pp. 1-18.

Recaps the civil rights career of Dr. King and his use of nonviolence as a means of achieving equal rights for blacks.

0757 "Comrade King?" Natl Rev, Vol. 35, November 11, 1983, p. 1382.

A discussion of King's Communist affiliation is revealed in this article.

0758 Cook, Samuel D. "Martin Luther King." J Negro Hist, Vol. 63, October, 1968, pp. 348-354.

Cook discusses the nature and personality of Dr. King at a Morehouse College class reunion.

0759 Coy, P. G. "Martin Luther King, Jr. and the Catholic Bishops' Peace Letter." Christ Century, Vol. 101, April 4, 1984, pp. 340-341.

Parallels the similarities between King's stance on the war in Vietnam and that of the Catholic Bishops' stance on the arms race.

0760 "The Crackdown." Nation. Vol. 201, October 11, 1965, pp. 205-206.

Looks at the consequences that King faced after speaking out against the war in Vietnam.

0761 Crawford, K. "Non-debate." Newsweek, Vol. 69, April 17, 1967, p. 46.

King calls for blacks to avoid military service in protest of the war in Vietnam.

0762 Danzig, D. "Meaning of Negro Strategy." Commentary, Vol. 37, February, 1964, pp. 41-46.

King is mentioned as just one of the elements that helped lead to blacks evolving as a viable force in American society.

0763 Dellums, R. V. "The Coalition's the Thing." Freedomways, Vol. 12, First Quarter, 1972, pp. 7-16.

Highlights the principles that Dr. King fought and died for.

0764 "Doctor King's Boycott." Sr Schol, Vol. 90, April 21, 1967, pp. 15-16.

Criticisms are rendered in response to King's boycott speech against the war in Vietnam.

0765 "Doctor King's Disservice to His Cause." Life, Vol. 62, April 2, 1967, pp. 4-5.

Criticizes Dr. King's stance on the Vietnam war.

0766 "Dr. King's Legacy." Commonweal, Vol. 88, April 19, 1968, pp. 125-126.

History has proved that the theory of nonviolence doesn't work, and King's tragic death helped to confirm that argument.

0767 "The Domestic Impact of the War in Vietnam." Drum Major, Winter, 1971, p. 14.

0768 "Dream Remains to be Fulfilled." Beijing R, Vol. 26, September 12, 1983, p. 12.

Contends that King's dream for freedom and equality for all remains unfilled.

0769 Edmund, T. "Martin Luther King and the Black Protest Movement.," Gandhi Mag, Vol. 20, January, 1976, pp. 235-249.

Examines King's ideology of Christian love and Gandhi's movement of nonviolence as a weapon for blacks in their struggles for equality.

0770 Epstein, Joseph. "Down the Line." Commentary, Vol. 40, October, 1965, pp. 101-105.

Dr. King and other black leaders express their views on social change in our society.

0771 "Execution of Dr. King." Ramp Mag, Vol. 6, May, 1968, p. 47.

Attacks the politicians that were responsible for criticizing King's philosophy of nonviolence and his anti-war statements about Vietnam.

0772 Fager, C. E. "Dilemma for Dr. King." Christ Century, Vol. 83, March 16, 1966, p. 331.

Analyzes the problems that King faces if he decides to come out against the war in Vietnam.

0773 "Farewell to a 'Drum Major for Justice and Peace.'" Freedomways, Vol. 8, Spring, 1968, pp. 101-102.

Defines King's importance to the civil rights movement.

0774 Galphin, Bruce M. "Political Future of Dr. King." Nation, Vol. 193, September 23, 1961, pp. 177-80.

Examines the power that King possesses with the black vote in the South.

0775 Golden, James L. "Black and White Political Allies in the Struggle for Freedom, 1941-1983." Negro Educ R, Vol. 36, January, 1985, pp. 22-40.

A. Philip Randolph, Martin Luther King and Bayard Rustin are a few of the leaders that helped to shape the civil rights movement.

0776 "A Good Journey to Martin Luther King, Jr." Liberation, Vol. 3, February, 1959, p. 19.

Comments on the impact of King's trip to India and the effect it could have on the civil rights movement.

0777 "Graham and King as Ghetto-Mates." Christ Century, Vol. 83, August 10, 1966, pp. 976-977.

Compares the likeness of Dr. King and Billy Graham in their philosophies on poverty and housing in America.

0778 Halberstam, D. "Martin Luther King, American Preacher." Esquire, Vol. 100, December, 1983, pp. 306-308+.

Contends that King was the driving force behind the civil rights movement, and his impact on the changes that were made are evident today.

0779 Halberstam, David. "Notes from the Bottom of the Mountain." Harper's, Vol. 236, June, 1968, pp. 40-42.

Reflects upon the character and ideology of Dr. King.

0780 Hall, Bob. "James Orange: With the People." South Expo, Vol. 9, Spring, 1981, pp. 110-116.

Reflects on the civil rights movement and mentions King's involvement and influence during that time.

0781 Hall, Grover C., Jr. "Alabama's Bus Boycott: What It's All About." US News World Rept, Vol. 41, August 3, 1956, pp. 83-87.

King and Hall discuss the pros and cons of the bus boycott.

0782 Halpern, Ben. "The Ethnic Revolt." Midstream, Vol. 17, January, 1971, pp. 3-16.

The involvement of Dr. King with the black revolutionary movement is mentioned in this discussion.

0783 Harding, V. "King and Revolution." Progressive, Vol. 47, April, 1983, pp. 16-17.

The notion of King calling for a new and larger movement against poverty is discussed.

0784 Harnett, Rodney. "Agreement With Views of Martin Luther King, Jr., Before and After His Assassination." Phylon, Vol. 33, Spring, 1972, pp. 79-87.

A survey showed that a majority of college and university board members agreed with the ideology of Dr. King.

0785 "Has Black Power Hurt Martin Luther King?" Sepia, Vol. 15, November, 196, pp. 14-18.

0786 Hatch, Roger D. "Racism and Religion: The Contrasting Viewsof Benjamin Mays, Malcolm X, and Martin Luther King, Jr." Jnl of Rel Thought, Vol. 20, Winter, 1980, pp. 26-36.

0787 Herberg, Will. "A Religious 'Right' to Violate the Law?" Natl Rev, Vol. 16, July 14, 1964, pp. 579-580.

Herberg feels that King's principles of civil disobedience do not coincide with the true Christian teachings of the Bible.

0788 "Hotter Fires." Newsweek, Vol. 62, July 1, 1963, pp. 19-21.

Criticizes King's method of attacking the racial problem.

0789 House, S. V. "Implications of Martin Luther King, Jr.'s Work and

Philosophy for Adult Education." Adult Lead, Vol. 25, April, 1977, pp. 229-30+.

Discusses the impact on King's philosophy in America and what it meant to the criteria for educating adults.

0790 Hughes, E. J. "Curse of Confusion." Newsweek, Vol. 69, May 1, 1967, p. 17.

Criticizes Dr. King's stand on the war in Vietnam.

0791 "'I Like the Word Black.'" Newsweek, Vol. 61, May 6, 1963, pp. 27-28.

Studies King's approach to the civil rights movement.

0792 "I Remember Martin." Ebony, Vol. 39, April, 1984, pp. 33-34+.

Friends close to the slain civil rights leader reflect on his personal character.

0793 King, Coretta. "He Had a Dream." Life, Vol. 67, September 12, 1969, pp. 54-54B+.

0794 "King Moves North." Time, Vol. 85, April 30, 1965, pp. 32-33.

King makes several speeches while in Boston on various civil rights matters.

0795 King, Mrs. Martin Luther. "'How Many Men Must Die?'" Life, Vol. 64, April 19, 1968, pp. 34-35.

Mrs. King reflects on her husband's past and reiterates his hope for peace and a society of nonviolence.

0796 "International Evening: Martin Luther King; Summary of Address." Publ Wkly, Vol. 191, June 19, 1967, p. 52.

Reviews a speech given by Dr. King in which he expresses his feelings on the topic of racism.

0797 "Is it All Right to Break the Law?" US News World Rept, Vol. 55, August 12, 1963, p. 6.

A synopsis of King's "Letter from a Birmingham Jail" is given.

0798 "Is Vietnam to Become a 'Civil Rights' Issue." US News World Rept, Vol. 59, July 19, 1965, p. 12.

Key civil rights leaders comment on King's stand against the war in Vietnam.

0799 Keller, Michael and Herberg, Will. "Early Christian Demonstrators, Dr. Herberg Replies." Natl Rev, Vol. 16, September 8, 1964, pp. 783-784.

Herberg gives additional justification as to why he feels King's teachings don't compare with the true teachings of Christianity.

0800 Kemper, J. S. "Doctor King's Policy: Invitation to Racial Violence? Excerpts from Address, September 21, 1965." US News World Rept, Vol. 69, October 4, 1965, p. 22.

King is accused of being the main culprit of mass crime through his philosophy of civil disobedience.

0801 "Kennedy to Mrs. King: Did a Phone Call Elect Kennedy President?" Negro Digest, Vol. 11, November, 1961, pp. 45-49.

The effects of whether a phone call to King's wife influenced the voter turn out of blacks is discussed.

0802 "King Acts for Peace." Christ Century, Vol. 82, September 29, 1965, p. 1180-1181.

Praises King for taking a stand against the war in Vietnam.

0803 King, C. S. "I Am Preparing Myself for My Husband's Death." Sepia, Vol. 16, November, 1967, pp. 48-49.

0804 King, Coretta. "He Had a Dream." Life, Vol. 67, September 19, 1969, pp. 83-86+.

0805 King, Coretta Scott and Gene Harper. "Keeping the Dream Alive." Soldiers, Vol. 39, January, 1984, pp. 25-26.

Mrs. King addresses several of Dr. King's ideologies concerning the civil rights movement.

0806 "King Wants White Demonstrators." Christ Century, Vol. 81, June 3, 1964, pp. 724-725.

Elaborates on the philosophy that blacks and whites must work together to bring about racial justice.

0807 Klein, M. "Other Beauty of Martin Luther King, Jr.'s 'Letter from a Birmingham Jail.'" Coll Comp and Comm, Vol. 32, February, 1981, pp. 30-37.

0808 Kotz, Nick. "Welfare Mothers and the Civil Rights Movement." Civ Lib Rev, Vol. 4, Nov./Dec. 1979, pp. 74-83.

Discusses a meeting in which King and the president of the welfare organization talk about various aspects of the civil rights movement.

0809 Lawrence, D. "Fallacy of Civil Disobedience." Read Digest, Vol. 87, October, 1965, pp. 111-12.

King gives his justification for defying an unjust law.

0810 Lawton, Rudy. "Lest We Forget: Tribute to Martin Luther King,

Jr." NJEA Rev, Vol. 56, January 20, 1983, pp. 18-20.

Concludes that King's achievements and philosophy could influence the school systems to become compassionate and sympathetic institutions.

0811 "The Legacy of Martin Luther King." Life, Vol. 64, April 19, 1968, p. 4.

The problems that can result in the fight for equal rights after the death of King are finally realized.

0812 Leonard, G. B. "Who Will Count His Woe?" Look, Vol. 32, August 20, 1968, p. 23.

Calls on the American people to remember and continue to carry out the deeds of Dr. King.

0813 Lubenow, G. C. "He Changed a Lot of things." Newsweek, Vol. 102, August 29, 1983, pp. 16-18.

Several people talk about the changes that were made in the South and mention King and his struggle for civil rights as an important part of this change.

0814 Mabee, Charles. "The Crisis in Negro Leadership." Antioch Rev, Vol. 24, Fall, 1964, pp. 365-378.

King is mentioned as one of the leaders who is still influential in the civil rights movement.

0815 McKissick, Floyd B. "Which Way for the Negro?" Newsweek, Vol. 69, May 15, 1967, pp. 27-28+.

King is mentioned as one of the civil rights leaders that is looked upon as having problems directing the movement at this point.

0816 "Malcolm X and Martin Luther King, Jr.: Violence Versus Non-Violence" Ebony, Vol. 20, April, 1965, pp. 168-169.

0817 "Man of the Year." Time, Vol. 83, January 3, 1964, pp. 13-16+.

An in-depth look at King and his philosophy in the events leading up to 1963.

0818 "The March's Meaning." Time, Vol. 122, October, 1983, p. 80.

King and other leaders interpret the purpose for the March on Washington.

0819 "Martin Luther King." Reporter, Vol. 38, April 18, 1968, pp. 10-12.

Studies the ideals of Dr. King and what he meant to the American people.

0820 "Martin Luther King, Jr. and Mahatma Gandhi." Negro Hist Bull, Vol. 31, May, 1968, pp. 4-5.

A comparison of King and Gandhi's philosophy of nonviolence is given and its impact on America and India.

0821 Meagher, Sylvia. "Two Assassinations." Min of One, Vol. 10, November, 1968, pp. 9-10.

The death of Dr. King was made possible through the racism and inhumanity that existed in American society.

0822 Mecartney, John M. "Civil Disobedience and Anarchy." Social Sci, Vol. 42, October, 1967, pp. 205-212.

Contends that the letter written by Dr. King in a Birmingham jail expresses the real meaning of civil disobedience and the law.

0823 Meyer, F. S. "Principles and Heresies." Natl Rev, Vol. 20, January 16, 1968, p. 36.

Expresses hopes that action is taken by the government to combat the revolutionary actions and ideology of Dr. King.

0824 "MLK's Tropic Interlude." Ebony, Vol. 22, June, 1967, pp. 112-14+.

King finishes his book Where Do We Go From Here while vacationing in Jamaica.

0825 "The Moderates' Predicament." Time, Vol. 91, April 19, 1968, p. 19.

Looks at King's ability as a leader among blacks in the U.S.

0826 "Montgomery Spectacle." America, Vol. 112, April 10, 1965, p. 474.

A summary of a speech given by Dr. King during the March on Montgomery is mentioned.

0827 Nelson, Harold A. "The Re-Education of Sociologists: A Note on the Impact of Dr. Martin Luther King, Jr. as Educator." J of Hum Rel, Vol. 16, 4th quarter, 1968, pp. 514-523.

Presents King's philosophies, and their impact on Sociologists and their studies of race relations.

0828 "New Tack for Dr. King; Broader Issues, Wilder Gosal." US News World Rept, Vol. 58, May 3, 1963, p. 18.

Reveals King's ambition to influence the world with his philosophy of human rights and peace.

0829 "No False Moves for King." Christ Century, Vol. 80, July 17, 1963, p. 99.

A comparison of Martin Luther and Dr. King is given.

0830 "Notes and Comments." New Yorker, Vol. 44, April 13, 1968, pp. 35-37.

A brief interview with King concerning threats on his life before his death and a look at the man in retrospect following his demise.

0831 Oates, Stephen B. "The Intellectual Odyssey of Martin Luther King." Mass Rev, Vol. 22, Summer, 1981, pp. 301-320.

A study of Dr. King with careful observation of his study and acceptance of Freud's ideologies.

0832 O'Connor, John J. "A Famous Letter." Community, Vol. 23, October, 1963, p. 10.

Comments on the importance of the letter that King wrote in response to public statements by several clergymen.

0833 "The Peaceful Kingdom." Natl Rev, Vol. 16, December 29, 1964, pp. 1135-1336.

During his stay in Oslo, King discusses his philosophy on several social issues.

0834 Pitre, M. "Economic Philosophy of Martin Luther King, Jr." Rev Black Pol Econ, Vol. 9, Winter, 1979, pp. 191-198.

Examines King's idea of economic justice and racial justice going hand in hand.

0835 Preace, H. "Hatred for Whites and Preachers Led to Stabbing of Martin Luther King." Sepia, Vol. 7, January, 1959, pp. 52-56+.

0836 "The Prince of Peace is Dead." Ebony, Vol. 23, May, 1968, p. 172.

Gives the reasons as to why King was known as a man of peace.

0837 Quarles, Benjamin. "Martin Luther King in History." Negro Hist Bull, Vol. 31, May, 1968, p. 9.

Expresses ideas that some day King will play an important part in American history.

0838 "Race Violence Will Defeat Itself." Christ Century, Vol. 75, September 17, 1958, p. 1046.

Explores King's tactics of using nonviolence as a means of achieving equal justice.

0839 Raines, J. C. "Righteous Resistance and Martin Luther King, Jr." Christ Century, Vol. 101, January 18, 1984, pp. 52-54.

Examines King's ability and philosophy as a key resister during the civil rights struggle.

0840 Rathburn, John W. "Martin Luther King: The Theology of Social

Action." Am Q, Vol. 20, Spring, 1968, pp. 38-53.

The author examines the origin and evolution of King's theological beliefs.

0841 Reed, Adolph L. Jr. "Strategy for a Communist Agenda: Civil Rights Equals Social Revolution." Phylon, Vol. 37, December, 1976, pp. 334-342.

Dr. King is labeled as having the ideology and characteristics of a Socialist.

0842 Richardson, Herbert W. "Martin Luther King . . . Unsung Theologian." Commonweal, Vol. 88, May 3, 1968, pp. 201-203.

Observations of Dr. King's ability as a theologian in dealing with social evils are made.

0843 Roberts, Adam. "Martin Luther King and Non-Violent Resistance." World Today, Vol. 24, June, 1968, pp. 226-236.

Examines King and the practice of nonviolence and the changes that were brought about in this practice after his death.

0844 Rowan, C. T. "Martin Luther King's Tragic Decision." Read Digest, Vol. 91, September, 1967, pp. 37-42.

The anti-Vietnam statements by Dr. King are criticized and analyzed in this article.

0845 Sellers, James E. "Love, Justice, and the Non-Violent Movement." Theol Today, Vol. 18, January, 1962, pp. 422-434.

Parallels the philosophy of Reinhold Niebuhr to that of Dr. King concerning the subject of racial justice.

0846 Sharma, Mohan. "Martin Luther King: Modern America's Greatest Theologian of Social Action." J Negro Hist, Vol. 53, July, 1968, pp. 57-63.

King's philosophy and a look at how these ideas were used in the movement are discussed.

0847 Sibley, M. "Martin King and the Future; Editorial." Liberation, Vol. 13, April, 1968, pp. 7-9.

Discusses an increased acceptance of King's ideology of nonviolence after his death.

0848 Smylie, James H. "On Jesus, Pharaohs, and the Chosen People: Martin Luther King as Biblical Interpreter and Humanist." Interpretation, Vol. 24, January, 1970, pp. 74-91.

Views King's use of the idea of exodus as a means for bringing about racial equality for blacks.

0849 Steinkraus, W. E. "Martin Luther King's Personalism and Non-Violence." J Hist Ideas, Vol. 34, January, 1973, pp. 97-111.

Contends that there is a strong connection between King the fighter for civil rights and King the contemplative philosopher.

0850 Sullivan, L. H. "Dreams of the Future." Negro Hist Bull, Vol. 46, January/February/March, 83, pp. 6-8.

Calls for a commitment from the American people to make Dr. King's dream of equaity for all a reality.

0851 Taussig, H. C. "America's Few." Eastern World, Vol. 19, November, 1964, pp. 5-6.

Mentions Dr. King as one of the few Americans that criticized the U.S. involvement in Vietnam.

0852 Templin, R. T. "Thoughts After the Assassination of Martin Luther King, Jr." J Hum Rela, 2nd Q, 1968, no p.

Addresses the death of Dr. King and the effect of his ideology on the conscience of man.

0853 "Top Man of the Negro 'Revolution.'" US News World Rept, Vol. 54, June 10, 1963, p. 21.

An overall view of what King has meant for blacks and their struggle for civil rights.

0854 VanderZanden, James W. "The Non-Violent Resistance Movement Against Segregation." Am J Sociol, Vol. 68, March, 1963, pp. 544-550.

Elaborates on King's philosophy of passive resistance as a tactic to end segregation against blacks.

0855 "Violence Versus Non-Violence." Ebony, Vol. 20, April, 1965, pp. 168-169.

A look at the similarities and differences of Malcom X and Dr. King.

0856 "Visions of the Promised Land." Time, Vol. 91, April 12, 1968, p. 20.

Brief highlights are given on various subjects King talked about throughout his life.

0857 "A Visit With Martin Luther King." Look, Vol. 27, February 12, 1963, pp. 92-96.

Examines King's work and influence in the civil rights movement and addresses his feelings on the progress of social justice in America.

0858 Wall, J. M. "King's Strength: The Power of Love." Christ Century, Vol. 100, January 26, 1983, p. 59.

Discusses the inception of King's acceptance of love as a viable force to bring about social change.

0859 Wasserman, L. D. "Legacy of Martin Luther King, Jr. Negro Hist Bull, Vol. 38, December, 1974, p. 333.

Alludes to Dr. King's philosophy of nonviolence as a means of making whites aware of their social conscience.

0860 "We Have Got to Deliver Nonviolent Results, Annual Convention." Newsweek, Vol. 68, August 22, 1966, pp. 58-59.

Addresses King's technique of nonviolence and the effects it had on whites and violent protest.

0861 Weaver, P. V. "Moral Education and the Study of United States History." Soc Educ, Vol. 39, January, 1975, pp. 36-39.

Dr. King's philosophy of nonviolence is used as a study guide to motivate children in the area of moral decisions.

0862 "Why They Riot." Natl Rev, Vol. 17, March 9, 1964, pp. 178-180.

Dr. King's tactics of nonviolence are labeled as a source of violence and rioting among blacks.

0863 "With But One Voice." Nation, Vol. 204, April 24, 1967, pp. 515-516.

Critics and allies of King speak against him for his public stance on the war in Vietnam.

0864 Willhelm, Sidney M. "Martin Luther King, Jr. and the Black Experience in America." J Black Stud, Vol. 10, September, 1979, pp. 3-19.

Discussion of King's ability as a scholarly writer and his talent to assess black-white relations in America are examined.

GOVERNMENT DOCUMENTS

0865 U.S. Congress, House. Representative B. Abzug speaking for "Martin Luther King, Jr." 93rd Cong., 1st Sess., Cong Rec, Vol. 119, April, 1973, p. H11281.

Request that funds be restored to the social programs that King envisioned as a part of the American dream.

0866 U.S. Congress, House. Representative J. Ashbrook remarks on "Rev. Martin Luther King: Man of Peace or Apostle of Violence." 90th

Cong., 1st Sess., Cong Rec, Vol. 113, October 4, 1967, pp. H27814-27827.

Believes that the true character of King is of violence and chaos. He proceeds by presenting facts to verify his claim.

0867 U.S. Congress, House. Representative Jonathan B. Bingham remarks on "Dr. Martin Luther King." 90th Cong., 1st Sess., Cong Rec, Vol. 113, April 5, 1967, p. H8497.

Expresses disappointment in Dr. King's anti-war speech on Vietnam.

0868 U.S. Congress, House. Representative J. Bingham comments on "Tragic Mistake of Dr. Martin Luther King." 90th Cong., 1st Sess., Cong Rec, Vol. 113, April 5, 1967, p. H8404.

Believes the speech made by Dr. King concerning the war in Vietnam could do harm to the peace settlement process.

0869 U.S. Congress, House. Representative H. Boggs remarks on "Episcopal Minister Blames Riot on King." 89th Cong., 1st Sess, Cong Rec, Vol. 111, September 3, 1965, p. H22888.

Reverend Watts disagrees with King's philosophy of civil disobedience.

0870 U.S. Congress, House. Representative John Conyers remarks on "The Development of Martin Luther King's Political and Social thought." 97th Cong., 1st Sess., Cong Rec, Vol. 127, May 14, 1981, pp. E2353-2354.

Includes a speech by David Garrow covering King's social and political philosophies.

0871 U.S. Congress, House. Representative John Conyers, Jr. remarks on "Martin Luther King as a Unifying Force." 97th Cong., 1st Sess., Cong Rec, Vol. 127, April 30, 1981, pp. E1991-1992.

Praises the seminars that were held across the country studying the philosophy of the late Dr. King.

0872 U.S. Congress, House. Representative John Conyers, Jr. "Martin Luther King, Jr. - Dreamer In Action." 97th Cong., 1st Sess., Cong Rec, Vol. 127, May 1, 1981, pp. E2030-E2031.

Remarks on King's philosophy of government and how it should work; submits a paper that examines King's role in the civil rights movement and his ability as a leader.

0873 U.S. Congress, House. Representative John Conyers, Jr. remarks on "Martin Luther King's Practice of Nonviolence." 97th Cong., 1st Sess., Cong Rec, Vol 127, May 5, 1981, pp. E2138-2139.

Contends that social action and racial justice can be achieved through the use of King's philosophy of nonviolence.

0874 U.S. Congress, House. Representative John Conyers remarks on "Martin Luther King's Theory and Practice of Civil Disobedience." 97th Cong., 1st Sess., Cong Rec, Vol. 127, May 13, 1981, pp. E2336-2337.

Studies King's philosophy of civil disobedience and the law.

0875 U.S. Congress, House. Representative Charles Diggs remarks on "Martin Luther King." 91st Cong., 1st Sess., Cong Rec, Vol. 115, April 3, 1969, p. H8734.

King was able to expose to the nation the suffering and injustice that poor people endured in our society.

0876 U.S. Congress, House. Representative Roy Dyson speaking for "King Remembered." 97th Cong., 1st Sess., Cong Rec, Vol. 127, January 27, 1981, p. E169.

Comments on the impact that King had on the rural communities, as well as those of the inner cities.

0877 U.S. Congress, House. Representative Don Edwards speaking for "Dr. Martin Luther King on Vietnam." 90th Cong., 1st Sess., Cong Rec, Vol. 113, May 2, 1967, pp. H11402-11406.

An analysis of King's views on Vietnam is given.

0878 U.S. Congress, House. Representative Don Edwards remarks on a "Statement of the California Farmer-Consumer Information Committee Honoring the Memory of Rev. Martin Luther King, Jr." 90th Cong., 2nd Sess., Cong Rec, Vol. 114, April 11, 1968, p. E9815.

Suggests that the nation pull together and carry out the teachings of Dr. King.

0879 U.S. Congress, House. Representative O. Fisher speaking against "The Linkup Between Civil Rights and Riots." 90th Cong., 1st Sess., Cong Rec, Vol. 113, August 7, 1967, pp. H21546-21548.

Comments on remarks by King concerning civil rights demands and violence.

0880 U.S. Congress, House. Representative O. Fisher remarks on "Those who Encourage Draft Dodging Should Be Jailed." 90th Cong., 1st Sess., Cong Rec, Vol. 113, May 9, 1967, p. E12204.

Contends that King and other leaders who constantly call for Americans to avoid the draft should be imprisoned and fined.

0881 U.S. Congress, House. Representative Foglietta speaking for "Martin Luther King's Birthday." 97th Cong., 2nd Sess., Cong Rec, Vol. 128, February 10, 1982, pp. E373-374.

Gives contrasting views on King's "Dream of Freedom" and that of President Reagan's dream of a "New Federalism."

0882 U.S. Congress, House. Representative Foglietta speaking for "Martin Luther King Birthday Bill." 98th Cong., 1st Sess., Cong Rec, Vol. 129, October 4, 1983, pp. H7887-7888.

Addresses the House and those in particular that discredited King as being a Communist.

0883 U.S. Congress, House. Representative R. Leggett speaking on "Meaning of the Life of Dr. Martin Luther King." 91st Cong., 1st Sess., Cong Rec, Vol. 115, June 5, 1969, pp. H14957-14972.

Disputes certain statements made by Representative Rarick discrediting King as a civil rights leader.

0884 U.S. Congress, House. Representative William Lehman remarks on "Behalf of Martin Luther King's Birthday." 93rd Cong., 1st Sess., Cong Rec, Vol. 119, January 15, 1973, p. E1111.

Comments on the unsolved socioeconomic problems that King addressed during his civil rights career.

0885 U.S. Congress, House. Representative Sander Levin remarks on "The March on Washington Revisited." 98th Cong., 1st Sess., Cong Rec, Vol. 129, September 12, 1983, p. E4181.

Looks at the changes that King brought about in our society.

0886 U.S. Congress, House. Representative Larry McDonald remarks on "The Spike in Reality - An Earlier Chapter in How the Soviets Funded American Communists." 97th Cong., 1st Sess., Cong Rec, Vol. 127, October 7, 1981, p. E4691.

Speculates that King had ties with the Communist Party.

0887 U.S. Congress, House. Representative James D. Martin remarks on "Martin Luther King on a Tightrope." 89th Cong., 1st Sess., Cong Rec, Vol. 111, May 26, 1965, p. A2665.

Discusses the off and on relationship between King and Johnson concerning different social issues.

0888 U.S. Congress, House. Representative John R. Rarick speaking against "The King and His Communists." 90th Cong., 2nd Sess., Cong Rec, Vol. 114, May 28, 1968, pp. E15471-15475.

Submits an article that supports the theory that King and the members of SCLC were pretenders.

0889 U.S. Congress, House. Representative John R. Rarick remarks on "Martin Luther King - A Study." 90th Cong., 2nd Sess., Cong Rec, Vol. 114, May 29, 1968, pp. E15651-15656.

Reviews three aspects of the life of King in an attempt to show that he was not as good as the public was led to believe.

0890 U.S. Congress, House. Representative John Rarick speaking against

"Saint Martin." 91st Cong., 2nd Sess., Cong Rec, Vol. 116, April 16, 1970, pp. E12290-12291.

Presents an article by G. S. Schuyler that discredits King as a civil rights leader.

0891 U.S. Congress, House. Representative Ben Reifel remarks on "Dr. King's Spirit Can Be Kept Alive." 90th Cong., 2nd Sess., Cong Rec, Vol. 114, April 8, 1968, p. E9253.

Continuing the objectives and programs of Dr. King would be one of the highest tributes that can be paid to the memory of his death.

0892 U.S. Congress, House. Representative W. Ryan speaking for "Memorial to Rev. Dr. Martin Luther King, Jr." 91st Cong., 1st Sess., Cong Rec, Vol. 115, April 3, 1969, pp. H8557-8558.

Views the life of King in regard to his civil rights struggle; includes a copy of the "Letter from a Birmingham Jail."

0893 U.S. Congress, House. Representative W. Ryan remarks on "Martin Luther King, Jr. and the Law." 90th Cong., 2nd Sess., Cong Rec, Vol. 114, June 13, 1968, p. H17108-17109.

Greenberg comments on King's ideas of civil disobedience and the law.

0894 U.S. Congress, House. Representative William Ryan remarks on "A Statement on the Death of Dr. Martin Luther King, Jr." 90th Cong., 2nd Sess., Cong Rec, Vol. 114, April 11, 1968, pp. E9847-9848.

0895 U.S. Congress, House. Representative J. Waggonner remarks on "Communist Investment in Martin Luther King is Paying Off Again." 90th Cong., 1st Sess., Cong Rec, Vol. 113, May 3, 1967, pp. H11639-11640.

King's constant protest is due to his strong Communist ties. Also contains excerpts of an anti-war Vietnam statement by King.

0896 U.S. Congress, House. Representative Waggonner comments on "Martin Luther King, Go Home." 89th Cong., 1st Sess., Cong Rec, Vol. 111, September 21, 1965, pp. H24634-24635.

Contends that King was not qualified to make statements regarding Vietnam nor any other matters referring to foreign matters.

0897 U.S. Congress, House. Representative Waggonner remarks on "Martin Luther King's Aid and Comfort to the Vietcong." 90th Cong., 1st Sess., Cong Rec, Vol. 113, April 5, 1967, p. H8474.

Analyzes Dr. King's speech concerning the war in Vietnam.

0898 U.S. Congress, House. Representative Walker remarks on "Congressmen Blast King on Red China Stand." 89th Cong., 1st Sess., Cong Rec, Vol. 111, September 20, 1965, p. A5300.

Comments on statements and activities by Dr. King concerning the war in Vietnam.

0899 U.S. Congress, House. Representative Prentiss Walker remarks on "Martin Luther King, Go Home." 89th Cong., 1st Sess., Cong Rec, Vol. 111, September 22, 1965, p. A5362.

0900 U.S. Congress, House. Representative Williams and Andrews speaking against "Martin Luther King, Jr." 89th Cong., 1st Sess., Cong Rec, Vol. 111, March 17, 1965, pp. H5307-5308.

Accuses King of being one of the most notorious gangsters of our generation.

0901 U.S. Congress, House. Representative Bob Wilson remarks on "Labor Attorney Raps Martin King." 89th Cong., 1st Sess., Cong Rec, Vol. 111, October 12, 1965, p. A5739.

Contends that King's philosophy of nonviolence only leads to chaos and disorder in society.

0902 U.S. Congress, House. Representative Lester Wolf remarks on "Long Island Catholic Sees Need for Racial Justice." 90th Cong., 2nd Sess., Cong Rec, Vol. 114, April 11, 1968, p. E9804.

Calls on Congress, the federal government, and the U.S. to complete King's dream for racial justice for all men.

0903 U.S. Congress, Senate. Senator W. Byrd remarks on "The Two Wars of Vietnam." 90th Cong., 1st Sess., Cong Rec, Vol. 113, April 17, 1967, p. S9804.

Criticizes Dr. King and other leaders for their constant remarks against Johnson and his policy toward Vietnam.

0904 U.S. Congress, Senate. Senator T. Dodd remarks on "Dr. Martin Luther King's Activities in Connection With U.S. Foreign Policy." 89th Cong., 1st Sess., Cong Rec, Vol. 111, September 15, 1965, p. S23908.

Believes that King's anti-Vietnam War statements should discontinue before they discredit him and the civil rights movement.

0905 U.S. Congress, Senate. Senator P. Hart remarks on "Interference With Civil Rights." 90th Cong., 2nd Sess., Cong Rec, Vol. 114, February 6, 1968, pp. S2264-2267.

Contains an article concerning King's reply to Johnson on the subject of the March on Washington.

0906 U.S. Congress, Senate. Senator T. McIntyre speaking for "The Accomplishments of President Johnson." 90th Cong., 1st Sess., Cong Rec, Vol. 113, April 18, 1967, p. S9917.

Claims Dr. King has weakened the civil rights movement by linking the movement with the war in Vietnam.

0907 U.S. Congress, Senate. Senator E. Muskie speaking for "Address By Hon. Frank M. Coffin in Honor of Dr. Martin Luther King, Jr." 90th Cong., 2nd Sess., Cong Rec, Vol. 114, April 24, 1968, p. S10500.

Addresses the various problems that King tried to solve and what we could do to carry out his deeds.

0908 U.S. Congress, Senate. Senator C. Percy speaking for "Martin Luther King and American Traditions." 91st Cong., 1st Sess., Cong Rec, Vol. 115, April 18, 1969, pp. S9625-9627.

Submits a speech on the obstacles that King faced in our society and the traditional values he embraced in order to carry out his fight for social justice.

0909 U.S. Congress, Senate. Senator S. Thurmond remarks on "Participation by Dr. Martin Luther King and Bayard Rustin in International Affairs." 89th Cong., 1st Sess., Cong Rec, Vol. 111, September 13, 1965, p. S23567.

Expresses his disappointment with the ambassador for speaking with King publicly on the subject of foreign affairs.

0910 U.S. Congress, Senate. Senator J. Tower comments on "Tribute to Senator Brooke." 90th Cong., 1st Sess., Cong Rec, Vol. 113, May 16, 1967, p. S12878.

Brooke feels that King is making a big mistake by equating the civil rights movement with the war in Vietnam.

0911 U.S. Congress, Senate. Senator J. Williams speaking for "Dr. King's Dream; Out National Obligation." 91st Cong., 1st Sess., Cong Rec, Vol. 115, April 3, 1969, pp. S8675-8676.

Contends that in order for King's dream to become a reality, it must be carried out by the entire nation and not fall on the shoulders of a few.

0912 U.S. Congress, Senate. Senator S. Young speaking for "Dr. Martin Luther King, Jr." 89th Cong., 1st Sess., Cong Rec, Vol. 111, September 16, 1965, pp. S24100-24101.

Defends Dr. King's right as a citizen with the right to express his views on the war in Vietnam.

0913 FBI Headquarters Files. Communist Party United States of America - Negro Question - Labor Movement. January 30, 1964, Washington, D.C.: FBI Headquarters Murkin Security Files, 2 p. (Mem. No. 296).

Mentions the ideology of King and SCLC and his hope of developing a program that would involve the labor movement.

0914 FBI Headquarters Files. Preparation of a Resolution on Vietnam. April 19, 1966, Washington, D.C.: FBI Headquarters Murkin Security Files, 2 p. (Int. Sec. No. 2468).

Information regarding SCLC's anti-war stance on Vietnam is discussed.

DISSERTATIONS & THESES

0915 Ausbrooks, Beth Nelson. "Muslims, Militants, Moderates: A Comparative Analysis on Black Power." Howard University, DAI, 1971, 33:793-A.

Dr. King is mentioned as one of the leaders whose ideology was examined.

0916 Benedetti, Robert R. "Ideology and Political Culture: The Civil Rights Movement and the American Creed, 1956-1969." University of Pennsylvania, DAI, 1975, 36:5505-5506-A.

A study of King and other black leaders' ideology is compared to that of the American system and belief.

0917 Blackwelder, Julia K. "Fundamentalist Reactions to the Civil Rights Movement Since 1954." Emory University, DAI, 1972, 33:1813-A.

White fundamentalists express their views about King and others on the subject of civil rights and civil disobedience.

0918 Burns, Emmett C. "Love, Power, and Justice as Central Elements is a View of Social Change: A Comparison and Evaluation of the Thought of Reinhold Niebuhr and Martin Luther King, Jr." University of Pittsburgh, DAI, 1974, 35:3047-A.

Examines the similarities and the significant differences in ideologies of King and Niebuhr.

0919 Carpenter, Joseph, Jr. "The Leadership Philosophy of Dr. Martin Luther King, Jr.: Its Educational Implications." Marquette University, DAI, 1970, 31:4280-A.

Dr. King's philosophy is reviewed as a tool or mechanism for solving social problems in our country.

0920 Garber, Paul Russell. "Martin Luther King, Jr.: Theologian and Precursor of Black Theology." Florida State University, DAI, 1973, 35:1212-A.

Seeks to prove that King was more than a civil rights activist and examines his theological ethic.

0921 Grice, Nurline H. "The Influence of Black Power on the Rhetorical Practices of Dr. Martin Luther King." Master's Thesis, Miami University, 1968.

A study of two of King's speeches and his change in rhetoric to meet the demands of the audience and the time.

0922 Hanigan, James Patrick. "Martin Luther King, Jr. and the Ethics of Militant Nonviolence." Duke University, DAI, 1974, 34:6095-A.

Examines the theological and philosophical background of King's belief in nonviolent resistance.

0923 Harper, Fredrick D. "Maslow's Concept of Self-Actualization Compared with Personality Characteristics of Selected Black Protesters. Martin Luther King, Jr., Malcolm X and Fredrick Douglass." Florida State University, DAI, 1971, 32:238-A.

The conditions in the lives of King and the others were considered to be close to Maslow's concept.

0924 Harris, John C. "The Theology of Martin Luther King, Jr." Duke University, DAI, 1974, 35:5515-5517-A.

King's theological preaching addresses the problems of black oppression in America.

0925 Holmes, James Leon. "What Shall We Be: A Study of the Political Thought of Three Black Americans." Duke University, DAI, 1980, 41:784-A.

Dr. King attempted to incorporate the ideologies of Booker T. Washington and DuBois along with his thoughts as a means to achieve equality for blacks.

0926 House, Secil V. "The Implications of Dr. Martin Luther King, Jr.'s Work and Philosophy for the Field of Adult Education." Indiana University, DAI, 1975, 36:6046-A.

Asks the question as to whether or not King's philosophy had any relevance to adult education.

0927 Jones, Nancy Baker. "Nonviolence to Revolution: the Ideological Evolution of Five Black Leaders." Master's Thesis, Texas Christian University, 1970.

Gives an analysis of King and several leaders regarding their philosophies on racial equality.

0928 Keele, Lucy A. M. "A Burkeian Analysis of the Rhetoric Strategies of Dr. Martin Luther King, Jr., 1955-1968." University of Oregon, DAI, 1972, 33:5869.

Examines whether King's style and content of speaking were consistent up until the time of his death.

0929 Lee, Shin Heang. "The Concept of Human Nature, Justice and Nonviolence in the Political Thought of Martin Luther King, Jr." New York University, DAI, 1980, 41:787-A.

An examination of King's ideas of justice and nonviolence as an integral part of social change is discussed.

0930 Luellen, David E. "Ministers and Martyrs: Malcolm X and Martin Luther King, Jr." Ball State University, DAI, 1972, 33:3548-A.

Outlines the philosophy and strategies of King and Malcolm X in their attempt to secure freedom and social justice for black in America.

0931 Maloney, Thomas S. "An Exposition and Critical Analysis of Theory of Nonviolence in the Writings of Dr. Martin Luther King, Jr." Master's Thesis, Catholic University.

An in-depth look at King's ideology of nonviolence as a weapon for ensuing peace and better race relations.

0932 Martin, S. Rudolph, Jr. "A New Mind: Changing Black Consciousness, 1950-1970." Washington State University, DAI, 1974, 35:3752-3753-A.

Alludes to the conflicts between King and Malcolm X in their approach to identifying black awareness.

0933 Marty, William Ray. "Recent Negro Protest Thought. Theories of Nonviolence and Black Power." Duke University, DAI, 1968, 29:3196-A.

Discusses King's advocacy for nonviolence as a way to bring about social action and and change in our society.

0934 Moore, Edward L. "Billy Graham and Martin Luther King, Jr.: An Inquiry Into White and Black Revivalistic Traditions." Vanderbilt University, DAI, 1979, 40:2123-A.

Analyzes the preaching styles of these two men and what they were hoping to achieve with their methods.

0935 Morris, William W. "Strategies for Liberation: A Critical Comparison of Martin Luther King, Jr. and Albert B. Cleage, Jr." Vanderbilt University, DAI, 1973, 34:5304-A.

A comparison on the philosophies of King and Cleage covering the areas of integration, violence and social institutions.

0936 Mullen, Robert William. "An Analysis of the Issues Developed by Select Black Americans on the War in Vietnam." Ohio State University, DAI, 1971, 32:4155-A.

This study mentions two of King's addresses concerning the war in Vietnam.

0937 McGregor, Marjorie. "Martin Luther King, Jr.: An Analysis of His Washington Speech." Master's Thesis, University of Oklahoma, 1965.

Explains the effectiveness of King's speech and how it was interpreted by black and white Americans.

0938 McGrigg, Lee Augustus. "Martin Luther King, Jr.: An Account of

His Civil Rights Movement in Alabama, 1955-65." Master's Thesis, Tennessee State University, 1969.

Examines King's philosophy and biographical outlook in three Alabama cities during a ten year period.

0939 Niccolls, S. Thomas. "The Nature and Function of Rhetorical Imagery: A Descriptive Study of Three Speeches by Martin Luther King." Master's Thesis, Ohio University, 1966.

Analysis of King's speeches and whether or not they displayed simile in their content. The appendix contains three of King's most well known speeches.

0940 Oglesby, Enoch H. "Ethical Implications of the Works of Selected Black Theologians: A Critical Analysis." Boston University, DAI, 1974, 34:5739-5740-A.

Compares King's theory of love and nonviolence as a tool for changing social structures to the philosophy of Reinhold Niebuhr.

0941 Onwubu, Chukwuemeka. "Black Ideologies and the Sociology of Knowledge: The Public Response to the Protest Thoughts and Teachings of Martin Luther King, Jr. and Malcolm X." Michigan State University, DAI, 1975, 36:4074-A.

Contrasts and comparisons are explored on the philosop½hies of King and Malcolm X.

0942 Payne, James Chris. "A Content Analysis of Speeches and Written Documents of Six Black Spokesmen: Fredrick Douglass, W.E.B. DuBois, Martin Luther King, and Malcolm X." Florida State University, DAI, 1970.

0943 Rudzka-Ostyn, Brygida I. "The Oratory of Martin Luther King and Malcolm X: A Study in linguistic stylistics." University of Rochester, DAI, 1972, 33:33457-A.

0944 Shelton, Robert Loren. "Black Revolution: The Definition and Meaning of Revolution in the Writings and Speeches of Selected Nationally Prominent Negro Americans, 1963-1968." Boston University Graduate School, DAI, 1970, 131:2488-A.

Dr. King and several other persons' writings are examined as a source of revolutionary literature in our society.

0945 Sloan, Rose Mary. "Then My Living Will Not Be in Vain: A Rhetorical Study of Dr. Martin Luther King, Jr., and the Southern Christian Leadership Conference in the Mobilization for Collective Action Toward Nonviolent Means to Integration, 1954-1964." Ohio State University, DAI, 1978, 38:4448-A.

A general view of this study is to analyze the nonviolent strategy used by King and SCLC in their fight for civil rights.

0946 Smith, Donald Hugh. "Martin Luther King, Jr.: Rhetorician of Revolt." University of Wisconsin - Madison, DAI, 1964, 25:3749-A.

Seeks to analyze the speaking and writing of Dr. King during the Montgomery boycott, Birmingham movement and March on Washington.

0947 Thompson, Joseph Milburn. "Martin Luther King, Jr. and Christian Witness: An interpretation of King Based on a theological Model of Prophetic Witness." Fordham University, DAI, 1981, 42:2180-A.

Intends to evaluate Dr. King and whether he meets the criteria to be considered prophetic.

0948 Turner, Otis. "Toward an Ethic of Black Liberation Based on the Philosophy of Martin Luther King, Jr., and Stokely Carmichael's Concept of Black Power." Emory University, DAI, 1974, 35:3114-3115-A.

A look at Dr. King's nonviolent practice and the causes of its limited success in civil rights struggle.

0949 Underwood, Willard Alva. "The Rhetoric of Black Orators: Perspectives for Contemporary Analysis." Bowling Green State University, DAI, 1972, 33:5873-A.

Dr. King and several other orators' speeches are analyzed in regard to their ideology on the civil rights movement.

0950 Walker, Douglas A. "The Thoreauvian Legacy of Martin Luther King." Master's Thesis, Texas Christian University, 1970.

A study of the relationship of Thoreau's political philosophy and that of Dr. King. Reveals the impact of Thoreau's ideology on King.

0951 Walton, Hanes, Jr. "The Political Philosophy of Martin Luther King, Jr." Howard University, DAI, 1967, 28:1875-1876-A.

Seeks to define the political ideology of King; he concludes that it is merely a politicl theology.

0952 Warren, Mervyn A. "A Rhetorical Study of the Preaching of Doctor Martin Luther King, Jr. Pastor and Pulpit Orator." Master's Thesis, Michigan State University, 1966.

Explores the variations of King's rhetoric as a minister and that of a civil rights leader.

0953 Wasserman, Lois D. "Martin Luther King, Jr.: The Molding of Nonviolence as a Philosophy and Strategy, 1955-1963." Boston University, DAI, 1972, 33:1666-A.

An analysis of the various elements which helped to develop King's ideology of nonviolence as a means to achieve equal rights for blacks.

0954 Watley, William Donnel. "Against Principalities: An Examination of Martin Luther King, Jr.'s Nonviolent Ethic." Columbia, University, DAI, 1980, 41:2154-A.

Describes nonviolence as a moral obligation of King and discusses the civil rights movement where he applied this belief.

0955 White, Clarence, Jr. "Doctor Martin Luther King, Jr.'s Contributions to Education as a Black Leader (1929-1968." Loyola University of Chicago, DAI, 1974, 35:2027-A.

This study tried to evaluate King's ideal of the civil rights movement and interpret its impact on education and growth in our society.

0956 Whitehead, Brady B., Jr. "Preaching Response to the Death of Martin Luther King, Jr." Boston University School of Theology, DAI, 1972, 33:2489-2490-A.

Compares several groups of ministers' attitudes toward Dr. King after his death.

0957 Willingham, Alex W. "The Religious Basis for Action in the Political Philosophy of Martin Luther King, Jr." Master's Thesis, University of Iowa, 1965.

A look at King's ideology and how he adapted it to real situations.

0958 Wilson, Oliver Wendell. "Black Leadership as a Phenomenom in the American Polity: A Dialectic Process." Claremont Graduate School, DAI, 1972, 32:5880-5881-A.

Autobiographical and biographical matters are discussed concerning King and other leaders and defining their roles as black leaders in American society.

0959 Zepp, Ira G., Jr. "The Intellectual Sources of the Ethical Thought of Martin Luther King, Jr., as Traced in His Writings with Special Reference to the Beloved Community." St. Mary's Seminary and University, DAI, 1971, 32:4101-4102-A.

Traces the influential background of King's trend of thought on social gospel and nonviolence.

Assassination

BOOKS

0960 Blumenthal, Sid, and Yazijian, Harvey, eds. _Government by Gunplay: Assassination Conspiracy Theories from Dallas to Today_. New York: New American Library, 1976.

Part I examines whether James Earl Ray was the only culprit in the assassination of King.

0961 The Committee to Investigate Assassinations. _American Political Assassinations: A Bibliography of Works Published 1963-1970 Related to the Assassination of John F. Kennedy, Martin Luther King, and Robert F. Kennedy_. Washington, D.C.: Committee to Investigate Assassinations, 1973.

A partial listing of books and journals discussing the death of Dr. King.

0962 _Congressional Quarterly Almanac_. Washington, D.C.: Congressional Quarterly Inc., 1979, Vol. 35, pp. 382-383.

The House Assassinations Committee conclude that King's death was linked to a conspiracy financed by a St. Louis businessman.

0963 _Congressional Quarterly Almanac_. Washington, D.C.: Congressional Quarterly Inc., 1978, Vol. 34, pp. 25, 210-213, 216.

Reviews the events and evidence that was presented at the public hearings on the assassination of Dr. King.

0964 Crotty, William J., ed. _Assassinations and the Political Order_. New York: Harper and Row, Pub., 1971.

A study of the attitudes and reactions of school children after the assassination of Dr. King.

0965 Donaldson, Norman and Donaldson, Betty. _How Did They Die?_ New York: St. Martins Pr., 1980.

Covers the events that lead to the assassination of Dr. King and a possibility of a conspiracy in the death of King is mentioned.

0966 Frank, Gerold. An American Death: The True Story of the Assassination of Dr. Martin Luther King, Jr. and the Greatest Manhunt of Our Time. New York: Doubleday and Company, Inc. 1972.

Presents the story of the assassination of King and covers specific material on the search for Ray and his trial.

0967 Gay, William T. Montgomery, Alabama, a City in Crisis. New York: Exposition Press, 1957.

Mentions the bombing episode that took place at Dr. King's home.

0968 Gilbert, Ben W., ed. Ten Blocks from the White House: Anatomy of the Washington Riots of 1968. New York: Frederick A Praeger, Pub., 1968.

Mentions the reaction of blacks in Washington when the death of King was announced.

0969 *Goode, Stephen. Assassination: Kennedy, King, Kennedy. New York: F. Watts, 1979.

Studies the possibilities of a conspiracy involving the deaths of King and the Kennedy brothers.

0970 *Haskins, James. The Life and Death of Martin Luther King, Jr. New York: Lothrop, Lee & Shepard, 1977.

Haskins discusses certain questions that were not answered about King's assassination.

0971 Huie, William Bradford. Did the FBI Kill Martin Luther King? New York: Thomas Nelson, Inc., 1977.

Gives updated information to prove that Ray acted alone in the assassination of Dr. King.

0972 Huie, William Bradford. He Slew the Dreamer. New York: Delacorte Press, 1968.

An in-depth study of the man that assassinated Dr. King and interviews with James Earl Ray.

0973 Knight, Janet M., ed. Three Assassinations: The Death of John and Robert Kennedy and Martin Luther King. New York: Facts on Files, Inc., 1971.

Examines the search for and consequent capture and trial of James Earl Ray.

0974 Knight, Janet M., ed. Three Assassinations: The Death of John and Robert Kennedy and Martin Luther King. New York: Facts on File, Inc., 1971.

Looks at the events surrounding the death of Dr. King and the type of reactions that were displayed by the U.S. and the world.

0975 Knight, Janet M., ed. Three Assassinations: The Death of John and Robert Kennedy and Martin Luther King. New York: Facts on File, Inc., 1978, Vol. 2.

Addresses the notion that there was a conspiracy involved in the assassination of Dr. King.

0976 Koch, Thilo. Fighters for a New World: John F. Kennedy, Martin Luther King, Robert F. Kennedy. New York: G. P. Putnam's Sons, 1969.

Reflections on the death of Dr. King are given.

0977 Lane, Mark and Dick Gregory. Code Name Zorro: The Murder of Martin Luther King, Jr. New Jersey: Prentice-Hall, Inc., 1977.

A look at King and the questionable circumstances surrounding his assassination.

0978 Leek, Sybil. The Assassination Chain. New York: Corwin Books, 1976.

Chapter Twelve reviews the assassination of Dr. King.

0979 McKinley, James. Assassination in America. New York: Harper and Row, 1977.

Chapter 7 reveals an in-depth look at the circumstances and events surrounding the assassination of Dr. King.

0980 McMillan, George. The Making of an Assassin: The Life of James Earl Ray. Boston: Little, Brown and Company, 1976.

Contains information on Ray's planned assassination of Dr. King.

0981 Miller, William Robert. Martin Luther King, Jr.: His Life, Martyrdom and Meaning for the World. New York: Weybright and Talley, Inc., 1968.

The events and activities that took place during King's assassination and the events that followed are reviewed.

0982 Newton, M. A Case of Conspiracy. California: Holloway House Publishing Co., 1980.

0983 Oates, Stephen B. Let the Trumpet Sound: The Life of Martin Luther King, Jr. New York: Harper & Row, Publishers, 1982.

Oates discusses the key events that led to the assassination of King. Also, he explores the reaction of blacks and whites to King's death.

0984 O'Neill, Daniel J., comp. Speeches by Black Americans.

California: Dickenson Pub. Co., 1971.

An analysis of what the assassination of Dr. King meant to the civil rights movement.

0985 Scott, Peter Dale. The Assassinations: Dallas and Beyond - A Guide to Cover-Ups and Investigations. New York: Vintage Bks., 1976.

Points out several factors that leads one to suspect that a conspiracy did exist in the killing of Dr. King.

0986 Sparrow, Gerald. Great Assassins. New York: Arco Pub., 1969.

Traces the events of the assassination of Dr. King and the manhunt for James Earl Ray that followed.

0987 Sween, Joyce A. and Blumberg, Rae Lesser. Reactions to the Assassination of President John F. Kennedy and Dr. Martin Luther King, Jr.; A Preliminary Report. Illinois: Northwestern University, 1969.

Contains a number of sociological data on the effects of Kennedy and King's assassination on the American public.

0988 Weisberg, Harold. Frame-up; The Martin Luther King/James Earl Ray Case. New York: Outerbridge & Dienstfrey, 1971.

Weisberg attempts to prove that Ray was not the actual shooter in the King assassination, but a decoy in a major conspiracy.

ARTICLES

0989 "Accident in Harlem." Time, Vol. 72, September 29, 1958, p. 14.

Accounts of the assassination attempt on King by a woman in a Harlem department store.

0990 "Accused Killer, a Clumsy Man with Closed Eyes." Life, Vol. 64, April 26, 1968, p. 42B.

Releases photographs of the suspect that was believed to be the person who killed King.

0991 "April was the Cruelest Month: All That Violence Didn't Have to Happen." Sch Mgt, Vol. 12, November, 1968, pp. 64-65+.

Reaction to civil disorders in public schools immediately after the death of Dr. King are discussed.

0992 "Assassins: Who Did It - and Why?" Newsweek, Vol. 73, March 24, 1969, pp. 28-29.

Looks at the deaths of Kennedy and King and ponders on the notion that a conspiracy existed in the killing of King.

0993 Chastain, W., Jr. "Assassination of the Reverend Martin Luther King, Jr. and Possible Links with the Kennedy Murders." Comp and People, Vol. 23, March, 1974, pp. 29-32.

Examines certain aspects of the death of King that might have presented a probable cause for a conspiracy.

0994 Clarke, James W. "How Southern Children Felt About King's Death." Trans-action, Vol. 5, October, 1968, pp. 35-40.

Studies the reaction of children to the death of King as compared to their reactions to the death of President Kennedy.

0995 Detwiler, B. "King; the Establishment Embrace." Liberation, Vol. 13, April, 1968, pp. 16-17.

Criticizes the comments made by he press concerning the life and death of King.

0996 "Dr. King's Murder: Nagging Questions Remain." US News World Rep, Vol. 66, March 24, 1969, p. 13.

The lack of evidence brought out at the trial of Ray still leaves the public wondering if a conspiracy existed in the death of King.

0997 "Dream - Still Unfulfilled." Newsweek, Vol. 73, April 14, 1969, pp. 34-35.

Events that took place following the death of King are viewed.

0998 Foreman, P. "Why James Earl Ray Murdered Dr. King; Against Conspiracy." Look, Vol. 33, April 15, 1969, pp. 104+.

0999 Gessell, J. M. "Memphis in Holy Week." Christ Cent, Vol. 85, May 8, 1968, pp. 619-20.

Reflects on the death of King and the impact it had on the city of Memphis and America.

1000 Hager, Barry. "House Move Reflects Questions on Cost of Assassination Probe." Cong Q W Rept, Vol. 35, January 8, 1977, pp. 46-48.

Reviews the details of the proposed budget for investigating the King and Kennedy assassinations.

1001 Hanes, A. J. "Why James Earl Ray Murdered Dr. King; for Conspiracy." Look, Vol. 33, April 15, 1969, pp. 104+.

Hanes concludes that Ray was given orders to kill Dr. King and presents reasons as to why he has drawn this conclusion.

1002 Hofstetter, C. Richard. "Political Disengagement and the Death of

Martin Luther King." Public Opinion Q, Vol. 33, Summer, 1969, pp. 174-179.

A discussion of the impact of Dr. King's assassination on blacks' political involvement is given.

1003 Holt, Don. "Was There a Plot on King?" Newsweek, Vol. 92, August 7, 1978, p. 21.

Discusses testimony by Russell Byers that two Missouri businessmen offered him money to arrange for King's death.

1004 Huie, W. B. "Story of James Earl Ray and the Plot to Assassinate Martin Luther King." Look, Vol. 32, November 12, 1970, pp. 96-97+.

An in-depth look at the man who assassinated King. Includes a full report of Ray's planning of and escape in the crime.

1005 "In Memoriam." Negro Digest, Vol. 17, August, 1968, p. 25.

Reveals the sympathetic outpouring of public grief concerning the death of Dr. King.

1006 "Incident in Harlem." Newsweek, Vol. 52, September 29, 1968, p. 24.

Dr. King is stabbed in a Harlem department store.

1007 "It May Be a Bell Tolling for Me." Newsweek, Vol. 71, April 22, 1968, pp. 23-24.

Studies the reaction to the death of King.

1008 "'It Really Doesn't Matter What Happens Now, I've Been to the Mountain Top.'" Life, Vol. 64, April 12, 1968, pp. 74-79.

Reveals photographs of Dr. King and the place or surroundings where he was assassinated.

1009 "JFK/MLK: Is There More to the Story?" Sr Schol, Vol. 109, November 18, 1976, pp. 9-10+.

Congress decides to reopen the assassination cases of John F. Kennedy and Dr. King.

1010 "James Earl Ray; The Man Who Killed Martin Luther King, Jr." Sepia, Vol. 17, July, 1968, pp. 76-77.

Takes an inside look at the man accused of assassinating Dr. King, along with theories as to how he was able to kill King and escape.

1011 "James Ray: Manhunt Ends, but Mysteries Remain." US News World Rept, Vol. 64, June 24, 1968, pp. 34-6.

Traces the search for and capture of James Ray, and discusses several issues that suggest that Ray wasn't the only person discusses involved.

1012 "Johnson, King and Ho Chi Minh." Christ Today, Vol. 12, April 26, 1968, pp. 24-25.

The death of King is discussed from a national and international viewpoint.

1013 Johnson, Lyndon B. "Dr. Martin Luther King, Jr." W Comp Pres Docs, Vol. 4, April 8, 1968, pp. 640-641.

The President proclaims a day of national mourning following the death of Dr. King.

1014 "Just How Many Stokleys?" Economist, Vol. 227, April 13, 1968, pp. 16-17.

Addresses the reaction of black and white extremists after the death of Dr. King.

1015 "King Assassination Revisited." Time, Vol. 107, January 26, 1976, pp. 16-18.

Doubts still persist concerning the lone assassin theory of the death of Dr. King.

1016 King, M. L., Sr. "Day They Killed My Son." McCalls, Vol. 105, April, 1978, pp. 33+.

Reveals a conversation held with Dr. King just prior to his assassination.

1017 Livernash, Bob. "House Panel Concludes Conspiracies Probably Part of Kennedy, King Deaths." Cong Q W Rept, Vol. 37, January 6, 1979, pp. 19-20.

The committee concludes that circumstances might have presented an opportunity for a conspiracy in King's death.

1018 "Lone Assassins." Time, Vol. 112, September 18, 1978, pp. 23-24.

The House Committee on Assassinations concludes that King was killed by a single assassin.

1019 McCombs, P. A. "It's So Beautiful to Be Black." Natl Rev, Vol. 20, April 23, 1968, p. 392.

A very brief reference is made about King and the impact that his death had on Washington, D.C.

1020 "The Man in Room 5." Time, Vol. 91, April 12, 1968, p. 21.

Gives speculations as to how Ray killed King and eventually escaped.

1021 Manis, Andrew M. "Silence or Shockwaves: Southern Baptist

Responses to the Assassination of Martin Luther King, Jr." Bapt Hist and Herit, Vol. 15, October, 1980, pp. 19-27+.

A discussion of leaders and laypersons responses on King's assassination is given, along with comments from Baptists concerning King's work.

1022 "Martin Luther King." Nation, Vol. 206, April 15, 1968, p. 490.

This editorial covers the impact of Dr. King's death on this country as a whole.

1023 "Martin Luther King Movement . . . One Year After His Death." Sepia, Vol. 18, April, 1969, pp. 8-10+.

The progress and future of the civil rights movement since King's death are examined.

1024 "Martyrdom Comes to America's Moral Leader." Christ Century, Vol. 85, April 17, 1968, pp. 475-476.

Reflects on the impact of King's death on our society and what the nation can do to fulfill King's dream.

1025 Meyer, Philip. "Aftermath of Martyrdom: Negro Militancy and Martin Luther King." Pub Opinion Q, Vol. 33, Summer, 1969, pp. 160-173.

A survey was conducted to test the theory that the King assassination increased black militancy.

1026 "Missing Its Man." Time, Vol. 112, August 14, 1978, p. 14.

The FBI files show that the agency failed to follow-up on a story involving the death of King.

1027 Montagno, M. "Who Killed the Dream." Newsweek, Vol. 86, December 8, 1975, p. 35.

The public calls for a reopening of the case concerning the death of Dr. King.

1028 "More Violence and War? - Effects of Dr. King Tragedy." US News World Rept, Vol. 64, April 15, 1968, p. 31-34.

Examines the effects of the spread of violence in cities across the U.S. after the assassination of King.

1029 Morganthau, Tom. "Tales of Conspiracy." Newsweek, Vol. 94, July 30, 1979, pp. 37-38.

The House Select Committee investigates the possibilities of plots involving James Ray's brothers and Ray's hope of claiming a bounty for killing King.

1030 "Mysteries in Case of Martin Luther King." US News World Rept,

Vol. 82, January 17, 1977, p. 30.

The House Committee on Assassination considers reopening the case involving the assassination of Martin Luther King.

1031 O'Leary, J. "Greatest Manhunt in Law Enforcement History." Read Dig, Vol. 93, August, 1968, pp. 63-69.

Reviews the search for an subsequent capture of the man who assassinated Martin Luther King.

1032 "One Man, One Gun?" Economist, Vol. 227, April 13, 1968, pp. 24-25.

The death of King will not affect the sale of handguns in the U.S.

1033 Parks, Gordon. "A Man Who Tried to Love Somebody." Life, Vol. 64, April 19, 1968, pp. 29-33.

Describes the funeral of Dr. King along with several photographs and raises questions about the feelings between whites and blacks following the death of King.

1034 "Publishers Rush New Issues of Dr. King's Books." Publ Wk, Vol. 193, April 15, 1968, p. 73.

Looks at the events that followed in the publishing sector following the assassination of Dr. King.

1035 "Rampage and Restraint." Time, Vol. 91, April 19, 1968, pp. 15-19.

Looks at the looting and arson that took place in the ghettos after King was killed.

1036 "Reactions to the Slaying of Martin Luther King." America, Vol. 118, April 20, 1968, pp. 534-36.

Reactions to the death of Dr. King abroad and in the U.S. are revealed in this article.

1037 Remington, Robin Alison. "Moscow, Peking and Black American Revolution." Survey, Vol. 74/75, Spring, 1970, pp. 237-252.

Mention attitude changes toward black Americans by the people of Moscow and Peking following the death of King.

1038 "Responsibility and Emotion." Time, Vol. 91, April 19, 1968, p. 60.

Reflections on the death of Dr. King and the impact it had on black and white Americans.

1039 "Riptide of Disunity." Bus Week, April 13, 1968, pp. 27-28.

King's death leaves the nation with a strong possibility of a major racial crisis.

1040 Romero, Patricia W. "Martin Luther King and His Challenge to White America." Negro Hist Bull, Vol. 31, May, 1968, p. 6.

An overview of the social implications involving King's death and race relations between whites and blacks.

1041 Schrag, Peter. "The Uses of Martyrdom." Saturday Rev, Vol. 51, April 20, 1968, pp. 28-29.

Attempts to explore the impact of Dr. King's life and his inevitable death on our society.

1042 "Seven Days in April: A Momentous Week Brings Hope for Peace -- Then National Tragedy." Newsweek, Vol. 71, April 15, 1968, pp. 26-30.

A brief look at the events that took place after the death of Dr. King was announced.

1043 "Shock." Life, Vol. 66, January 10, 1969, pp. 30-32.

The effects of King's assassination on America society is evaluated.

1044 Siegel, L. S. "Childrens' and Adolescents' Reactions to Assassination of King, ML." Devel Psychol, Vol. 13, March, 1977, pp. 284-285.

A majority of the children felt that King was killed for a personal motive, and not because of a basic ideology.

1045 Slater, J. "Five Years After." The Garbage Workers. "Memphis and Dr. King." Ebony, Vol. 28, April, 1973, pp. 46-48+.

Looks at the impact of Dr. King's movement and death on the sanitation workers and blacks in the city of Memphis.

1046 Smith, Baxter. "FBI Memos Reveal Repression Schemes." Black Scholar, Vol. 5, April, 1974, pp. 43-48.

Reveals information that links the government to the deaths of Dr. King and Malcom X.

1047 Sprague, R. E. "Assassination of Reverend Martin Luther King, Jr., the Role of James Earl Ray, and the Question of Conspiracy." Comput Auto, Vol. 19, December, 1970, pp. 44+.

1048 Stokes, L. "Who and What Killed Dr. Martin Luther King, Jr.?" Ebony, Vol. 36, April, 1981, pp. 76-79+.

Concludes that James Earl Ray killed King and that Dr. King was most likely the victim of a conspiracy.

1049 "Supposition, House Report on Assassination is Short on Hard Evidence." Time, Vol. 114, July 30, 1979, p. 30.

The House Select Committee concludes that the assassination of King warrants speculation of a probably conspiracy.

1050 "Troubled Nation Adds Up the Loss." Bus Week, April 13, 1968, p. 29.

Several people express their views concerning the death of Dr. King.

1051 Turner, W. W. "Some Disturbing Parallels." Ramp Mag, Vol. 6, June 29, 1968, pp. 33-36.

Discusses the conflicting reports of the Attorney General and the available evidence on the Kennedy-King assassination.

1052 Turner, W. W. "Some Disturbing Parallels." Ramp Mag, Vol. 7, January 25, 1969, pp. 127-129.

1053 Wainwright, Loudon. "Some Uncomfortable Questions." Life, Vol. 64, April 26, 1968, p. 266.

Expresses ideas of uncertainty among whites and their sincerity about civil rights following the death of King.

1054 "Who Killed King?" Newsweek, Vol. 71, April 22, 1968, pp. 31-33.

An inside look at the investigation that followed after the death of King and the subsequent identity of the suspect.

1055 "Who Killed the Dream?" Newsweek, Vol. 86, December 8, 1975, p. 35.

There are calls for the reopening of investigations into the murder of King after it was revealed that the FBI had submitted to harassing tactics.

1056 "Widening Search." Time, Vol. 91, April 19, 1968, p. 20.

The authorities continue their search for the assassin of Dr. King.

1057 Woodbury, Richard. "Murder Clues: Handprints, a Car Chase and a Silly Smile." Life, Vol. 64, April 19, 1968, p. 40.

Details the exact actions of Ray just minutes before King was shot and describes the events that followed.

GOVERNMENT DOCUMENTS

1058 U.S. Congress, House. Investigation of the Assassination of Martin Luther King, Jr., Vol. 1, 1978, (CIS No. 79-H961-8).

Examines the first phase of investigations following the death of King.

1059 Investigation of the Assassination of Martin Luther King, Jr., Vol. 2, 1978 (CIS No. 79-H961-9).

Focuses on Ray's arrival in Memphis during the same time King was there.

1060 Investigation of the Assassination of Martin Luther King, Jr. Vol. 4, 1978 (CIS No. 79-H961-10).

This hearing covers the final cross examination of Ray's testimony regarding the death of King.

1061 Investigation of the Assassination of Martin Luther King, Jr., Vol. 4, 1978 (CIS No. 79-H961-11).

Investigates the support of federal and state law enforcement during and after the assassination of King.

1062 Investigation of the Assassination of Martin Luther King, Jr., Vol. 5, 1978 (CIS. No. 79-H961-19).

This document explores the notions that Ray had help in escaping after the assassination of Dr. King.

1063 Investigation of the Assassination of Martin Luther King, Jr., Vol. 6, 1978 (CIS No. 79-H961-20).

The Committee examines charges brought against the FBI regarding their subversive activities against Dr. King.

1064 Investigation of the Assassination of Martin Luther King, Jr., Vol. 7, 1978 (CIS No. 79-H961-21).

This volume looks at the possibility of a murder contract on Dr. King that was issued by a St. Louis, Mo. based on segregationist group.

1065 Investigation of the Assassination of Martin Luther King, Jr., Vol. 8, 1978 (CIS No. 79-H961-22).

Examines James Earl Ray and his brothers' involvement in a bank robbery. Ray supposedly financed his assassination of King through the use of this robbery.

1066 Investigation of the Assassination of Martin Luther King, Jr., Vol. 9, 1979 (CIS No. 79-H961-23).

Interviews with James Earl Ray concerning the assassination of King.

1067 Investigation of the Assassination of Martin Luther King, Jr., Vol. 10, 1979 (CIS No. 79-H961-24).

A second in a series of interviews held with Ray concerning the death of King.

1068 Investigations of the Assassination of Martin Luther King, Jr., Vol. 11, 1979 (CIS No. 79-H961-25).

The final in a series of talks that were held with James Earl Ray at the state penitentiary.

1069 U.S. Congress, House. Investigation of the Assassination of Martin Luther King, Jr., Vol. 12. 95th Cong., 2nd Sess., Washington, D.C.: Congressional Information Service, Inc., 1979 (CIS No. 79-H961-26).

This document reveals letters and notes written by Ray concerning his assassination activities of Dr. King.

1070 U.S. Congress, House. Investigation of the Assassination of Martin Luther King, Jr., Vol. 13. 96th Cong., 1st Sess., Washington, D.C.: CIS, Inc., 1979 (CIS No. 79-H961-35).

Contains report findings involving firearms, fingerprints and polygraph examinations of James Earl Ray.

1071 U.S. Congress, House. Legislative and Administrative Reform, Vol. 2: Appendix to Hearings. 95th Cong., 2nd Sess., Washington, D.C.: CIS, Inc., 1978 (CIS No. 79-H961-33).

Examines the FBI's responsibilities in its protection for the safety of Dr. King.

1072 U.S. Congress, House. Select Committee on Assassinations. Committee Meetings. 95th Cong., 1st Sess., Washington, D.C.: CIS, Inc., 1977 (CIS No. 77-H961-6).

Discusses several meetings that were held on the selections of committee members and a budget for continuing investigations into the death of King.

1073 U.S. Congress, House. Select Committee on Assassinations. Compilation of the Staements of James Earl Ray. 95th Cong., 2nd Sess., H. Rpt. 1080, Washington, D.C.: Congressional Information Service, Inc., 1978 (CIS No. 78-H963).

This article covers a series of interviews with Ray, which includes his escape from prison and his arrest after the assassination of Dr. King.

1074 U.S. Congress, House. Select Committee on Assassinations. Creating a Select Committee on Assassinations. 95th Cong., 1st Sess., H. Rpt. 3. Washington, D.C. CIS, Inc., 1977, (CIS No. 77-H683-1).

Reports on a resolution that would get up a committee to study the events surrounding the assassination of King and Kennedy.

1075 U.S. Congress, House. Select Committee on Assassinations. Final Report, Summary of Findings and Recommendations. 95th Cong., 2nd Sess., H. Rpt. 1828. Washington, D.C.: CIS, Inc., 1978 (CIS

No. 78-H953-7).

The Committee presents its findings and makes recommendations about the assassination of Dr. King.

1076 U.S. Congress, House. Select Committee on Assassinations. Report of the Select Committee on Assassinations, U.S. House of Representatives. 96th Cong., 1st Sess., H. Rept. 1828, p. 2. Washington, D.C.: CIS, Inc., 1979 (CIS No. 79-H963-1).

This report contains information on the possibility of a conspiracy involving the death of Dr. King.

1077 U.S. Congress, House. Select Committee on Assassinations. Report of the Select Committee on Assassinations. 95th Cong., 1st Sess., H. Rept. 119. Washington, D.C.: CIS, Inc., 1977 (CIS No. 77-H963-2).

Reviews the presentation of new evidence in the King and Kennedy inquiries.

1078 U.S. Congress, House. Select Committee on Assassinations. Report Together with Additional and Supplemental Views of the Select Committee on Assassinations. 91th Cong., 2nd Sess., H. Rpt. 1781. Washington, D.C.: Congressional Information Service, Inc., 1976 (CIS No. 76-H963-6).

This document reports on the progress made by the Committee on Assassination of the death of Dr. King. Also, it recommends that this committee continue with its investigation.

1079 U.S. Congress, House. Representative G. Brown remarks on "Joint Select Congressional Committee to Investigate Questions Raised by Assassinations of Dr. Martin Luther King, Jr. and senator Robert F. Kennedy." 90th Cong., 2nd Sess., Cong Rec, Vol. 114, July 18, 1968, pp. H22126-22128.

Examines the accusations that a conspiracy existed in the assassination of Dr. King.

1080 U.S. Congress, House. Representative J. Corman remarks on "The Aftermath of Tragedy." 90th Cong., 2nd Sess., Cong Rec, Vol. 114, April 11, 1968, pp. E9764-9965.

Addresses the problem of violence and disorder following the assassination of Dr. King.

1081 U.S. Congress, House. Representative James Corman comments on "We Are Called Upon to Make a Beginning in the Struggle for Civil Rights." 90th Cong., 2nd Sess., Cong Rec, Vol. 114, April 10, 1968, p. H9531.

In the wake of King's assassination the Representative calls for the passage of the Fair Housing Bill.

1082 U.S. Congress, House. Representative Leonard Farbstein remarks on

"Dr. Martin Luther King." 91st Cong., 1st Sess., Cong Rec, Vol. 115, April 3, 1969, pp. E8737-8738.

Feels that the justice department should not close the case on King's death because there are too many unanswered questions concerning the case.

1083 U.S. Congress, House. Representative R. Ichord remarks on "King Murder Hatched Abroad." 90th Cong., 2nd Sess., Cong Rec, Vol. 114, May 9, 1968, p. H12621.

Theorizes that King's death was a part of a plot by Cuba and China.

1084 U.S. Congress, House. Representative Jacobs remarks on "America Has Lost Another Battle in the War Against Hate." 90th Cong., 2nd Sess., Cong Rec, Vol. 114, April 8, 1968, p. H9164.

Comments on what blacks and whites should do to combat the death of Dr. King.

1085 U.S. Congress, House. Representative Joseph M. McDade remarks on "Dr. Martin Luther King." 90th Cong., 2nd Sess., Cong Rec, Vol. 114, July 30, 1968, pp. 24363-24364.

Comments on the attitudes of people in relation to the assassination of King.

1086 U.S. Congress, House. Representative Robert H. Michel remarks on "Day of Mourning." 90th Cong., 2nd Sess., Cong Rec, Vol. 114, April 11, 1968, p. E9731.

Contends that all whites should not be held accountable for the death of King, but closer observance should be made of the looters and rioters in our cities.

1087 U.S. Congress, House. Representative Hugh Scott remarks on "Past and Present Wounds." 90th Cong., 2nd Sess., Cong Rec, Vol. 114, April 10, 1968, p. E9647.

Pleads with the country to end the violence that took place following the death of King and to work towards love and understanding in the communities.

1088 U.S. Congress, House. Representative Bob Wilson remarks on "Memorialization of Vietnam War Dead." 90th Cong., 2nd Sess., Cong Rec, Vol. 114, April 9, 1968, p. E9380.

Suggests that the flag should not be flown at half staff for King alone, but for the servicemen who were killed in Vietnam as well.

1089 U.S. Congress, House. Representative Lester L. Wolf remarks on "League of Women Voters on Dr. King's Death." 90th Cong., 2nd Sess., Cong Rec, Vol. 114, April 11, 1968, pp. E9796-9797.

Accuses all white Americans for the death of Dr. King and calls for constructive action by everyone to fight for the end of discrimination.

1090 U.S. Congress, Senate. Senator Bayh comments on "An Unfinished Symphony." 91st Cong., 1st Sess., Cong Rec, Vol. 115, April 3, 1969, p. S8673.

Hopes that the death of King will help to unite the nation and enable the nation to work toward justice and freedom for everyone.

1091 U.S. Congress, Senate. Senator Byrd remarks on "Editorial on the Death of Dr. King." 90th Cong., 2nd Sess., Cong Rec, Vol. 114, April 17, 1968, pp. S9876-98.

The majority of looting and rioting following King's death was due to his doctrine of every man's having the right to disobey the law.

1092 FBI Headquarters Files. Assassination of Martin Luther King, Jr., April 5, 1968, Washington, D.C.: FBI Headquarters Murkin Security Files, 2 p. (Tel. No. 184).

Talks about the weapon and a bag that was left at the scene of the shooting where King was killed.

1093 FBI Headquarters Files. The Attorney General with Consideration of Information About the Arrest of Ray. April 22, 1968, Washington, D.C.: FBI Headquarters Murkin Security Files, 2 p. (Letter No. 1823).

Considers several possibilities of how James Earl Ray was able to assassinate King and escape.

1094 FBI Headquarters Files. Chicago Illinois; Threat to Kill Martin Luther King, March 17, 1965. March 17, 1965, Washington, D.C.: FBI Headquarters Murkin Security Files, 1 p. (Encl. No. 1038).

Involves a conversation with a man who states he is going to kill Dr. King.

1095 FBI Headquarters Files. Dr. Martin Luther King, Jr. July 18, 1975, Washington, D.C.: FBI Headquarters Murkin Security Files, 6 p. (Mem. No. 3965).

Studies King's movement from one hotel to another prior to his death and includes a statement by Abernathy discussing the events that took place on the day King was killed.

1096 FBI Headquarters Files. Eric Galt. April 11, 1968, Washington, D.C.: FBI Headquarters Murkin Security Files, 4 p. (Mem. No. 859).

Covers an intensive search for a man by the name of Galt who was seen leaving the area where King was killed.

1097 FBI Headquarters Files. Hoover. April 7, 1968, Washington, D.C.: FBI Headquarters Murkin Security Files, 3 p. (Airtel No. 146).

Shows approximately forty-seven photos of the area where King was shot in Memphis.

1098 FBI Headquarters Files. Identification of James Earl Ray. April 9, 1968, Washington, D.C.: FBI Headquarters Murkin Security Files, 4 p. (Mem. No. 1395).

A press release discloses that Ray is the suspect wanted in the fatal shooting of King.

1099 FBI Headquarters Files. J. G. Robinson Considered as Suspect. April 9, 1968, Washington, D.C.: FBI Headquarters Murkin Security Files, 2 p. (Tel. No. 14).

Considers the man that attacked King in a Selma hotel as a logical suspect in the King assassination.

1100 FBI Headquarters Files. Letter Questioning Protection Afforded Dr. Martin Luther King on July 24, 1964 by FBI Agents. August 18, 1964, Washington, D.C.: FBI Headquarters Murkin Security Files, 1 p. (Encl. No. 435).

The FBI is questioned about the legalities of protecting King against assassination attempts.

1101 FBI Headquarters Files. Memphis to Hoover. April 8, 1968, Washington, D.C.: FBI Headquarters Murkin Security Files, 6 p. (Tel. No. 223).

Information concerning the car that was used by the suspect who assassianted King is given.

1102 FBI Headquarters Files. Murder of Martin Luther King, Jr. April 5, 1968, Washington, D.C.: FBI Headquarters Murkin Security Files, 1 p. (Rept. No. 2).

Covers a report sent to various government officials detailing the assassination of King and mentions a key suspect by the name of John Willard.

1103 FBI Headquarters Files. Threats Against Martin Luther King, Jr. October 22, 1964, Washington, D.C.: FBI Headquarters Murkin Security Files, 1 p. (Mem. No. 494).

The FBI outlines the procedures that should be used whenever there is a threat to kill King.

1104 FBI Headquarters Files. Unknown Subject; Also Known as John Willard; Martin Luther King, Jr. - Victim; Civil Rights. April 5, 1968, Washington, D.C.: FBI Headquarters Murkin Security Files, 2 p. (Mem. No. 174).

Examines the bullet taken from King's body in order to determine the actual weapon that was used.

1105 FBI Headquarters Files. Unknown Subject; Dr. Martin Luther King

(Deceased) - Victim Civil Rights. April 4, 1968, Washington, D.C.: FBI Headquarters Murkin Security Files, 5 p. (Mem. No. 327).

Detailed information is given of the events that followed after King was shot in Memphis. Such things as lab reports and probable suspects are revealed.

1106 FBI Headquarters Files. Unknown Subject; Martin Luther King, Jr. - Victim Civil Rights. April 5, 1968, Washington, D.C.: FBI Headquarters Murkin Security Files, 1 p. (Mem. No. 177).

The complete findings on the actual rifle that killed King are given.

1107 FBI Headquarters Files. Unknown Subjects; Threats to Assassinate Martin Luther King, Jr., March 6-9, 1965. March 16, 1965, Washington, D.C.: FBI Headquarters Murkin Security Files, 1 p. (Mem. No. 1035).

Several death threats are called in to various FBI offices to assassinate King when he marches from Selma to Montgomery.

Commemorations and Eulogies

BOOKS

1108 Congressional Quarterly Almanac. Washington, D.C.: Congressional Quarterly Inc., 1981, Vol. 37, p. 403.

The House agrees to finance a bust of the late Dr. King.

1109 Congressional Quarterly Almanac. Washington, D.C.: Congressional Quarterly Inc., 1982, Vol. 38, p. 533.

The Senate passes a resolution calling for a statue or bust of King to be placed in the capital.

1110 Congressional Quarterly Almanac. Washington, D.C.: Congressional Quarterly Inc., 1979, Vol. 35, pp. 584.

Discusses the action on a bill that would make King's birth day a national holiday.

1111 Congressional Quarterly Almanac, Washington, D.C.: Congressional Quarterly Inc., 1983, Vol. 39, pp. 21, 600-602, 6-C.

Reagan signs into a law a bill making Martin Luther King's birthday a legal public holiday. Also includes background information on this public law.

1112 Knight, Janet M., ed. Three Assasinations: The Death of John and Robert Kennedy and Martin Luther King. New York: Facts on File, Inc., 1971.

A brief description of King's funeral service is given.

1113 Mays, Benjamin E. Disturbed About Man. Richmond: John Knox Press, 1969.

The complete text of the eulogy for Dr. King as delivered by Dr. B. F. Mays is given.

1114 Merriam, Eve. I Am a Man: Ode to Martin Luther King. Garden City: NY: Doubleday, 1971.

A poetic tribute to King and his fight for equal rights.

1115 Metcalf, George R. Black Profile. New York: McGraw-Hill, 1970.

Views the death of King and the tribute paid to him at his funeral.

1116 Petrie, Paul James. The Leader; for Martin Luther King, Jr. Rhode Island: Hellcoat Press, 1968.

A tribute to King and his struggle for racial justice is expressed in this poem.

1117 Searle, John D. Twentieth Century Christians. Edinburgh: Saint Andrews Press, 1977.

An excerpt of the eulogy delivered at King's funeral is mentioned in Chapter 9.

1118 Webb, Robert N. Leaders of Our Time. New York: Franklin Watts, Inc., 1965.

Briefly mentions that King was awarded the Nobel Peace Prize.

ARTICLES

1119 Alpern, D. M. "Behind the King Debate." Newsweek, Vol. 102, October 31, 1983, p. 32.

Senator Helms campaigns against making King's birthday a national holiday.

1120 "An American Tragedy; State Troopers Charge Marching Negroes at Selma, Ala." Newsweek, Vol. 65, March 22, 1965, pp. 18-21.

Events that cumulated at the Montgomery march and King's participation are mentioned.

1121 "Anniversary of the Birth of Dr. Martin Luther King, Jr." Weekly Comp of Pres, Vol. 19, January 24, 1983, pp. 63-64.

Reagan addresses the accomplishments of King in the area of civil rights.

1122 "As 150,000 Said Farewell to Dr. King." US News World Rept, Vol. 64, April 22, 1968, pp. 38-39.

King is laid to rest in Atlanta.

1123 Barrett, C. O. "Tribute." NY State Ed, Vol. 55, May, 1968, p. 6.

Excerpts of a memorial ceremony for Dr. King is given.

1124 Belafonte, Harry. "Martin Luther King and W.E.B. DuBois: A Personal Tribute." Freedomways, Vol. 12, First Quarter, 1972, pp. 17-21.

Pays homage to two civil rights leaders and their fight for equal justice.

1125 Bims, H. "Sculptor Looks at Martin Luther King." Ebony, Vol. 28, April, 1973, pp. 95-96+.

A discussion of a statue of Dr. King that was unveiled in the city of Chicago.

1126 "Birthday Celebration for MLK." Ebony, Vol. 36, March, 1981, pp. 126-129.

Covers a rally of more than 100,000 persons calling for a national holiday for King.

1127 Booker, S. "Katie Hall Leaves House but Claims in King bill and Vows to Return." Jet, Vol. 67, December 3, 1984, pp. 38-40.

Looks at the Congresswoman who was instrumental in making the King holiday a reality.

1128 Breindel, Eric. "King's Communist Associates." New Repub, Vol. 190, January 30, 1984, p. 14.

Helms suggests that King was influenced in his actions by Communists, and the proposed bill for a national holiday should be given careful consideration before passage.

1129 Brennecke, Harry E. "Memorial to Dr. King." Negro Hist Bull, Vol. 31, May, 1968, p. 8.

A poem written for the death of the late Dr. King.

1130 Campbell, B. M. "A National Holiday for a King." Black Enterp, Vol. 14, January, 1984, p. 21.

An inside look at the legislative action that took place over 15 years involving the passage of a national holiday for King.

1131 "Children's Tribute to Dr. Martin Luther King, Jr." Negro Hist Bull, Vol. 31, May, 1968, p. 2.

Children of an elementary school express their loss of Dr. King through poems and paragraphs.

1132 Church, G. J. "A National Holiday for King." Time, Vol. 122, October 31, 1983, p. 32.

Discusses Senator Helms' smear tactics of accusing King of being a Communist sympathizer.

1133 "Coretta King Upset by Holiday Date Chosen for MLK in Georgia." Jet, Vol. 67, December 10, 1984, p. 7.

The governor of Georgia has decided to celebrate King's birthday the day after Thanksgiving and not the third Monday in January.

1134 "Dr. King Lives on in Bronze." Sepia, Vol. 17, November, 1968, p. 69.

American sculptor dedicates a bust in memory of the late Dr. King.

1135 Garrow, D. J. "The Helms Attack on King." South Expos, Vol. 12, Mr/April, 1984, pp. 12-15.

An in-depth look at the methods and material Helms tried to use to block the passage of a bill honoring Dr. King.

1136 "House OKs Commission to Oversee New King Holiday." Jet, Vol. 66, August 13, 1984, p. 8.

The 31 member commission will assist in the organization of the first observance honoring Dr. King.

1137 Howard, R. "Requiem to Dr. Martin Luther King, Jr." Negro Hist Bull, Vol. 32, April, 1969, p. 17.

A tribute to the late Dr. King and his fight for civil rights.

1138 Jordon, M. "In Silent Tribute." Black Enterp, Vol. 10, June, 1980, pp. 58-61.

The city of Charlotte erects a life-sized statue in honor of the late Dr. King.

1139 "King Center Commemorates the March on Washington [1963 March]." Jet, Vol. 67, September 17, 1984, p. 27.

Entertainers help celebrate the 21st anniversary of King's historic March on Washington.

1140 "King Center in Atlanta Preparing Teaching Tool on Life, Words of MLK." Jet, Vol. 65, January 16, 1984, p. 12.

1141 "King Day." Newsweek, Vol. 75, January 26, 1970, pp. 24+.

The importance of a national holiday for King is discussed.

1142 "King Holiday - New Law's Effect." US News World Rept, Vol. 95, October 31, 1984, p. 13.

Explains the ruling on the holiday bill that was established in honor of King.

1143 "King's Birthday Salute Includes Tribute to His Aide Who is Now Major." Jet, Vol. 65, January 30, 1984, pp. 6-8.

1144 "King's Last March." Time, Vol. 91, April 19, 1968, pp. 18-19.

Details the funeral procession of Dr. King.

1145 "King's Last March: 'We Lost Somebody.'" Newsweek, Vol. 71, April 22, 1968, pp. 26-31.

Describes the funeral services of Dr. King.

1146 Leavy, Walter. "A Living Memorial to the Drum Major for Justice." Ebony, Vol. 38, August, 1983, pp. 124+.

Examines the completion of the MLK Center for Nonviolent Social Change and its current financial situation.

1147 "Martin Luther King: Honored, but Still Controversial." Economist, Vol. 289, October 22, 1983, pp. 23-24.

Arch-conservatives fight in the Senate to block the passage of a national holiday honoring King.

1148 "Martin Luther King, Jr., Center for Social Change: A Monument to a Martyr." Ebony, Vol. 29, April, 1974, p. 126-130.

Addresses the initial phase of the construction of the Center for Social Change in honor of the late Dr. King.

1149 "Martin Luther King, Jr., and His Dream." Learning, Vol. 11, January, 1983, pp. 50-58+.

Contains a series of learning posters and other material on the life and contributions of Dr. King.

1150 "Martin Luther King Will Have His Day." US News World Rept, Vol. 95, October 17, 1983, p. 16.

Looks at the proposed vote in the Senate that would make King's birthday a national holiday.

1151 Mays, Benjamin, E. "Eulogy." Negro Hist Bull, Vol. 31, May, 1968, p. 24.

Calls on all of goodwill to pray for those that might have hatred in their hearts and to continue to work towards the completion of King's goals.

1152 "National Afro-American (Black) History Month, February 1984." Weekly Comp of Pres, Vol. 20, February 6, 1984, pp. 156-158.

Reagan mentions his signing into law a national holiday marking the birthday of Dr. King.

1153 "A National Holiday for Martin Luther King?" US News World Rept, Vol. 95, August 29, 1983, p. 49.

Two representatives give pro and con views on whether there should be a national holiday for King.

1154 Nuby, Charlotte. "He Had a Dream." Negro Hist Bull, Vol. 31, May, 1968, p. 21.

A poem written by a ninth grade student eulogizing the death of King.

1155 "Poetry Honors Dr. Martin Luther King." El Eng, Vol. 52, January, 1975, p. 108.

Several elementary school children express their feelings towards Dr. King through poetry.

1156 LaKritz, G. G. "Martin Luther King, Jr." Instructor, Vol. 78, March, 1969, p. 80.

A choral reading honoring the death of Dr. King is given.

1157 Rothman, Robert. "Congress Clears King Holiday After Heated Senate Debate." Cong Q W Rept, Vol. 41, October 22, 1983, pp. 2175-2179.

Covers the background and debate on the holiday bill that was passed by the Senate.

1158 Shevitz, L. "What Manner of Man; Choral Reading for Martin Luther King Day; January 15." Instructor, Vol. 86, January, 1977, p. 140.

1159 "Still On: Dr. King's March." US News World Rept, Vol. 64, April 29, 1968, p. 10.

Part of the Poor People's March entailed pulling mule drawn wagons symbolizing the death of Dr. King.

1160 Strauss, E. A. "Martin Luther King; Song." Instructor, Vol. 79, January, 1970, p. 75.

Includes a copy of the words and music.

1161 Tancil, Sallie E., ed. "A Children's Tribute to Dr. Martin Luther King, Jr." Negro Hist Bull, Vol. 31, March, 1968, p. 2.

A group of elementary school kids express their sorrow about the death of Dr. King.

1162 Thomas, C. W. "Nobel Peace Prize Goes to Martin Luther King." Negro Hist Bull, Vol. 28, November, 1964, p. 35.

This editorial expresses some feelings by certain people regarding King being named the winner of the Nobel Peace Prize.

1163 Topkins, S. B. "Dr. Martin Luther King, Jr.; Poem." Instructor, Vol. 80, January, 1971, p. 82.

1164 Wonder, S. "For Dr. King - A Holiday." Essence, Vol. 12,

Urges everyone interested in supporting a holiday for King to join the March on Washington which will support legislation for such a King holiday.

1165 Wonder, S. "Happy Birthday." Ebony, Vol. 39, January, 1984, pp. 70-71.

Words of a song in honor of the late Dr. King are given.

1166 "Year of Homage to Martin Luther King." Ebony, Vol. 24, April, 1969, pp. 31-34+.

Lists the numerous memorials, statues, tributes, and honors bestowed upon King following his assassination.

1167 Yevtushenko, Y. "In Memory of Dr. Martin Luther King." Negro Hist Bull, Vol. 31, May, 1968, p. 14.

A poem written in memory of Dr. King.

GOVERNMENT DOCUMENTS

1168 U.S. Congress, House. Authorizing a Bust or Statue of Martin Luther King, Jr. to Be Placed in the Capitol. 95th Cong., 1st Sess., H. Rpt. 486, Washington, D.C.: CIS, Inc., 1977 (CIS No. 77-H423-9).

The report discusses the recommendations of a resolution to place a statue of Dr. King in the Capitol.

1169 U.S. Congress, House. Authorizing a Bust or Statue of Martin Luther King, Jr. to be Placed in the Capitol. 97th Cong., 1st Sess., H. Rpt. 217, Washington, D.C.: CIS, Inc., 1981, (CIS No. 81-H423-2).

Continues to study the possibility of designating a statue of King in the nation's Capitol.

1170 U.S. Congress, House. Bicentennial Coinage, Commemorative Medals, Commemorative Coins, Grants to Eisenhower College from Coinage Receipts. 93 Cong., 1st Sess., Washington, D.C.: CIS, Inc., 1973 (CIS No. 73-H241-8).

This hearing authorizes the distribution of a silver dollar and determines that the MLK Center for Social Change would act as the vendor of this coin.

1171 U.S. Congress, House. Designation of the Birthday of Martin Luther King, Jr. as a Legal Public Holiday. 98th Cong., 1st Sess., H. Rept. 3345. Washington, D.C.: CIS, Inc., 1983 (CIS No. H623-4).

Recommends that the third Monday in January of each year be made a public holiday to honor the birth of King.

1172 U.S. Congress, House. Medals in Commemoration of Dr. Martin Luther King, Jr. 95th Cong., 2nd Sess., H. Rpt. 13643. Washington, D.C.: CIS, Inc., 1978 (CIS, No. 78-H243-20).

An agreement between the Treasury Department and the Martin Luther King Center for Social Change is hoped to be reached for the purpose of manufacturing medals.

1173 U.S. Congress, House. Subcommittee on Census and Population. Designate the Birthday of Martin Luther King, Jr. as a Legal Public Holiday. 94th Cong., 1st Sess., Washington, D.C.: CIS, Inc., 1975 (CIS No. 76-H621-43).

Hears arguments to establish the birthdate of Dr. King as a national holiday.

1174 U.S. Congress, House. Subcommittee on Census and Population. Proposals for Martin Luther King, Jr. National Holiday. 97th Cong., 2nd Sess., Washington, D.C.: CIS, Inc., 1982 (CIS No. 82-H621-22).

Hearings cover support and opposition on the subject of designating King's birthday as a national holiday.

1175 U.S. Congress, House. Subcommittee on Historic Preservation and Coinage. To Provide for the Striking of National Medals in Commemoration of: Dr. Martin Luther King, Jr. and the XIII Olympic Winter Games. 95th Cong., 2nd Sess., Washington, D.C.: CIS, Inc., 1978 (CIS No. 78-H241-54).

Proposes to produce 500,000 medals to commemorate the life of King.

1176 U.S. Congress, Senate. Authorizing a Bust or Statue of Martin Luther King, Jr. to be Placed in the Capitol. 96th Cong., 1st Sess., S. Rpt. 543, Washington, D.C.: CIS, Inc., 1979 (CIS No. 79-S683-14).

Considers the authorization of acquiring a bust of King that would be placed in the Capitol.

1177 U.S. Congress, Senate. Authorizing the Joint Committee on the Library to Procure a Bust or Statue of Dr. Martin Luther King, Junior to be Placed in the Capitol. 97th Cong., 2nd Sess., H. Con. Res. 153. Washington, D.C.: CIS, Inc., 1982 (CIS No. 82-5683-12).

Seeks authorization to obtain a bust or statue of King for viewing in the Capitol.

1178 U.S. Congress, Senate. Martin Luther King, Jr. National Holiday, S. 25. 96th Cong., 1st Sess., S. Rpt. 25. Washington, D.C.: CIS, Inc., 1980 (CIS No. 80-S521-6).

The committee reviews background material on King and hears supportive testimony from Andrew Young, Conyers, Coretta King, and others.

1179 U.S. Congress, Senate. Subcommittee on Parks, Recreation, and Renewable Resources. Martin Luther King, Jr., National Historic Site, State of Georgia; and the Chacoan Culture Preservation Act. 96th Cong., 2nd Sess., Washington, D.C.: CIS, Inc., 1980 (CIS No. 81-S311-40).

Hears testimony in support of establishing an historic site for King in Atlanta.

1180 U.S. Congress, House. Representative Bella Abzug remarks on "Children Petition for Martin Luther King Day." 93rd Cong., 1st Sess., Cong Rec, Vol. 119, January 26, 1973, p. H9532.

The signatures of over three thousand petitions by school children are obtained.

1181 U.S. Congress, House. Representative John Anderson remarks on "Dr. Martin Luther King, Jr." 93rd Cong., 1st Sess., Cong Rec, Vol. 119, January 15, 1973, pp. E1104-1105.

Commemorates the anniversary of Dr. King through a series of quotes from his various writings.

1182 U.S. Congress, House. Representative I. Andrews speaking for "Passage of Martin Luther King, Jr. National Holiday." 98th Cong., 1st Sess., Cong Rec, Vol. 129, August 2, 1983, p. H6214.

Calls on Congress to accelerate their work on the passage of a bill honoring King.

1183 U.S. Congress, House. Representative L. Aucoin remarking on "Martin Luther King's Values and Beliefs." 98th Cong., 1st Sess., Cong Rec, Vol. 129, August 3, 1983, pp. H6467-6470.

Supports his resolution to establish a federal holiday honoring King with a copy of the Letter from Birmingham City Jail."

1184 U.S. Congress, House. Representative Jonathan B. Bingham remarks on "A Eulogy." 90th Cong., 2nd Sess., Cong Rec, Vol. 114, April 23, 1968, pp. E10382-10383.

Submits the test of a eulogy by Rabbi Taragin honoring the death of King.

1185 U.S. Congress, House. Representative Bingham speaking for "Martin Luther King Statue." 91st Cong., 2nd Sess., Cong Rec, Vol. 116, October 14, 1970, pp. H36756-36757.

A list of the members of Congress that are in favor of having a bust or statue of King placed in the Capitol is included.

1186 U.S. Congress, House. Representative George E. Brown reiterates

"Dr. King's Utopic Dream." 98th Cong., 1st Sess., Cong Rec, Vol. 129, August 2, 1983, p. E3917.

Gives an account of King's hope for a co-existence of all races. Believes that the passage of the holiday bill would allow this dream to live on.

1187 U.S. Congress, House. Representative Yvonne Burke remarks on "Memory of Dr. Martin Luther King and Senator Robert F. Kennedy." 93rd Cong., 1st Sess., Cong Rec, Vol. 119, March 15, 1973, p. E8304.

Includes a song written in honor of the late Dr. King and Senator Kennedy.

1188 U.S. Congress, House. Representative Phillip Burton remarks on "Martin Luther King." 91st Cong., 1st Sess., Cong Rec, Vol. 115, April 2, 1969, p. E8473.

Comments on the first anniversary of the death of Dr. King.

1189 U.S. Congress, House. Representative Daniel E. Button remarks on "Black Thursday, April 4, 1968." 90th Cong., 2nd Sess., Cong Rec, Vol. 114, April 23, 1968, pp. E10381-10382.

Submits a poem that pays tribute to the death of Dr. King.

1190 U.S. Congress, House. Representative Carroll A. Campbell inserts, "Letter to the President." 98th Cong., 1st Sess., Cong Rec, Vol. 129, September 20, 1983, p. E4416.

Reads a letter sent to the President asking for his signing for a legislation that would honor King's birthday as a national holiday.

1191 U.S. Congress, House. Representative Cardiss Collins speaking for "Authorizing A Bust or Statue of Martin Luther King, Jr. to be Placed in the Capitol." H. Con. Res. 153, 97th Cong., 1st Sess., Cong Rec, Vol. 127, September 15, 1981, p. E4220.

Praises the House of its support to place a bust of Dr. King in the halls of Congress.

1192 U.S. Congress, House. Representative J. Conyers speaking for "Designating the Birthday of Martin Luther King, Jr. as a Legal Holiday." 91st Cong., 1st Sess., Cong Rec, Vol. 115, February 26, 1969, pp. H4536-4537.

Comments on the letters and petitions that were received in favor of a national holiday for Dr. King.

1193 U.S. Congress, House. Representative Conyers speaking for "The Martin Luther King Holiday Bill." 92nd Cong., 1st Sess., Cong Rec, Vol. 117, February 10, 1971, pp. H2338-2340.

Includes several state proclamations that are in support of honoring King's birthday as a national holiday.

1194 U.S. Congress, House. Representative Conyers speaking in "Praise of the Subcommittees Responsible for the Mark-up of the Martin Luther King Holiday Bill." 98th Cong., 1st Sess., Cong Rec, Vol. 129, June 30, 1983, p. H4810.

Pays tribute to the committees responsible for hearing testimonies on a bill honoring King.

1195 U.S. Congress, House. Representative Conyers speaking for "Rediscovering Dr. King's Legacy for the 1980s." 97th Cong., 1st Sess., Cong Rec, Vol. 127, April 1, 1981, pp. H1261-1263.

Discusses a series of seminars and sit-ins to be held throughout the country honoring King and his teachings. Statements by Mrs. King and agendas are given for these events.

1196 U.S. Congress, House. Representative John Conyers inserts "Statement of Prof. George Wald Supporting the birthday of Martin Luther King as a Federal Holiday." 98th Cong., 1st Sess., Cong Rec, Vol. 129, June 23, 1983, p. E3147.

Includes a letter that expresses a need for a national holiday honoring King.

1197 U.S. Congress, House. Representative William Coyner inserts, "Pittsburgh City Council Resolution." :97th Cong., 1st Sess., Cong Rec, Vol. 127, January 22, 1981, p. H157.

Requests Congress to establish King's birthdate as a national holiday.

1198 U.S. Congress, House. Representative E. Daddario remarks on "Proclamation of the State of Connecticut." 91st Cong., 1st Sess., Cong Rec, Vol. 115, December 12, 1969, p. E38955.

Proclaims the birthday of King to be Martin Luther King Day in the state of Connecticut.

1199 U.S. Congress, House. Representative T. Dulski remarks on "Proposal to Honor the Late Dr. Martin Luther King." 91st Cong., 2nd Sess., Cong Rec, Vol. 116, January 22, 1970, pp. E879-880.

The city of Buffalo proposes to rename an expressway in honor of the late Dr. King.

1200 U.S. Congress, House. Representative Don Edwards remarks on "Memory of Martin Luther King, Jr." 91st Cong., 2nd Sess., Cong Rec, Vol. 116, December 19, 1970, pp. E42829-42830.

Inserts of two resolutions calling for King's birthday to become a national holiday.

1201 U.S. Congress, House. Representative W. E. Fauntroy remarks on "Martin Luther King, Jr. Birthday." 92nd Cong., 1st Sess., Cong Rec, Vol. 117, July 31, 1971, p. E28599.

Hopes to have a bill passed that would make King's birthday a legal holiday in the District of Columbia.

1202 U.S. Congress, House. Representative Paul Findley remarks on "Memorial at Lincoln's Tomb." 90th Cong., 2nd Sess., Cong Rec, Vol. 114, April 22, 1968, p. E10241.

Mentions the sermon that was given at the tomb honoring the death of the late Dr. King.

1203 U.S. Congress, House. Representative Hamilton Fish, Jr. "Martin Luther King, Jr.: A Tribute." 97th Cong., 1st Sess., Cong Rec, Vol. 127, January 16, 1981, p. E64.

Fish pays tribute to the late Dr. King and requests that his birthday be made a public holiday.

1204 U.S. Congress, House. Representative Garcia speaking for "Continued Bipartisanship Urged Toward Passage of Martin Luther King Birthday Holiday Bill." 98th Cong., 1st Sess., Cong Rec, Vol. 129, August 4, 1983, p. H6480.

Applauds the work of Republicans and Democrats in the House on the passage of King's bill, and asks that the members of the Senate and the President take the same initiative.

1205 U.S. Congress, House. Representative Robert Garcia speaking for "Proposed Legislation." 97th Cong., 2nd Sess., Cong Rec, Vol. 128, February 23, 1982, p. E47.

Statement presented to the Census Subcommittee regarding the designation of King's birthday as a national holiday.

1206 U.S. Congress, House. Representative Robert Garcia speaking for "Statue of Martin Luther King, Jr." H. Con. Res. 153, 97th Cong., 1st Sess., Cong Rec, Vol. 127, September 23, 1981, pp. E4395-5396.

Remarks on the adoption of a bill to place a bust of King in the Capitol; however, he feels that this in not enough and a national holiday is still the main goal.

1207 U.S. Congress, House. Representative Benjamin A. Gilman. "Dr. Martin Luther King - A Great American." 97th Cong., 1st Sess., Cong Rec, Vol. 127, January 16, 1981, pp. E58-59.

Informs the House that King's birthday has not become a reality and action should be taken on this bill.

1208 U.S. Congress, House. Representative S. Hall speaking for "Passage Designation of the Birthday of Martin Luther King, Jr. As a Legal Public Holiday." H. R. 3706, 98th Cong., 1st Sess., Cong Rec, Vol. 129, August 2, 1983, pp. H6235-6269.

Covers testimonies for and against the passage of a bill honoring Dr. King.

1209 U.S. Congress, House. Representative J. Hanley remarks on "Thoughts of Parishioners of St. Bartholomew's Church, Bethesda, MD on Dr. King." 90th Cong., 2nd Sess., Cong Rec, Vol. 114, April 8, 1968, p. H9166.

Memorial thoughts for the late Dr. King are revealed in this eulogy.

1210 U.S. Congress, House. Representative Augustus Hawkins remarks on "Deep in our Hearts." 90th Cong., 2nd Sess., Cong Rec, Vol. 114, May 22, 1968, p. E14561.

Includes an article from the AFL-CIO honoring King for his fight in the area of fair labor.

1211 U.S. Congress, House. Representative F. Horton comments on "Honoring the Late Reverend Martin Luther King." 91st Cong., 1st Sess., Cong Rec, Vol. 115, February 26, 1969, p. H4540-4541.

Includes several letters from elementary school students requesting that King's birthday be made a national holiday.

1212 U.S. Congress, House. Representative William Hudnut, III remarks on "A National Holiday on Dr. Martin Luther King's Birthday." 93rd Cong., 1st Sess., Cong Rec, Vol. 119, January 24, 1973, p. E2165.

Feels that a holiday for King would symbolize an appreciation for other minority groups and their contributions to America throughout history.

1213 U.S. Congress, House. Representative Barbara Jordan remarks on "In Memoriam: Martin Luther King, Jr." 93rd Cong., 1st Sess., Cong Rec, Vol. 119, April 4, 1973, p. E11094.

Comments on the anniversary of the death of the late Dr. King.

1214 U.S. Congress, House. Representative Jack F. Kemp remarks on "President Reagan and Mrs. King on Martin Luther King's Birthday: Commemorating the Civil Rights Revolution." 98th Cong., 1st Sess., Cong Rec, Vol. 129, November 4, 1983, pp. E5332-5333.

Remarks are made concerning the signing into law of a national holiday honoring King.

1215 U.S. Congress, House. Representative Dale E. Kildee, "Eloquent Support Expressed for National Holiday Honoring Rev. Martin Luther King, Jr." 97th Cong., 1st Sess., Cong Rec, Vol. 127, 1981, pp. E183-184.

Gives an account of King's contributions to the world and why a national holiday should be made in his honor.

1216 U.S. Congress, House. Representative G. Long speaking for the "Bill That Designates King's Birthday as a National Holiday." H.R. 800, 98th Cong., 1st Sess., Cong Rec, Vol. 129, July 14, 1983,

p. E3506.

1217 U.S. Congress, House. Representative Allard Lowenstein remarks on "Martin Luther King." 91st Cong., 1st Sess., Cong Rec, Vol. 115, April 3, 1969, pp. E8734-8735.

Robert Kennedy comments on the death of Dr. King.

1218 U.S. Congress, House. Representative R. Madden remarks on "Martin Luther King: Birthday Anniversary." 93rd Cong., 1st Sess., Cong Rec, Vol. 119, January 15, 1973, p. E1093.

Pays tribute to King on the anniversary of his birthday.

1219 U.S. Congress, House. Representative Madden speaking for "Martin Luther King's Birthday: A National Holiday." 91st Cong., 2nd Sess., Cong Rec, Vol. 116, March 3, 1970, pp. H5776-5777.

The city of Gary petitions Congress to declare the birthday of Dr. King a national holiday.

1220 U.S. Congress, House. Representative Spark M. Matsunaga remarks on "Dr. Martin Luther King, Jr." 90th Cong., 2nd Sess., Cong Rec, Vol. 114, April 25, 1968, p. E10760.

A former judge pays tribute to the late Dr. King through a poem.

1221 U.S. Congress, House. Representative R. R. Mazzoli speaking for "Passage of Martin Luther King, Jr. National Holiday." H.R. 800, 98th Cong., 1st Sess., Cong Rec, Vol. 129, June 30, 1983, p. E3336.

Contends that passage of this bill will never let us forget what King did for the idea of social change.

1222 U.S. Congress, House. Representative Abner Mikva comments on "New Black Unity: Dr. King Holiday." 91st Cong., 1st Sess., Cong Rec, Vol. 115, January 23, 1969, p. E1706.

Comments on a bill that was introduced to designate Dr. King's birthday as a national holiday.

1223 U.S. Congress, House. Representative Anthony Toby Moffett. "The Martin Luther King Day March: Some Observations." 97th Cong., 1st Sess., Cong Rec, Vol. 127, January 27, 1981, p. E174.

These remarks are critical of the small participation by whites in the march for King's holiday and the poor coverage by the media of this event.

1224 U.S. Congress, House. Representative Jim Moody speaking for "Designation of the Birthday of Martin Luther King, Jr. as a Legal Holiday." H.R. 3706, 98th Cong., 1st Sess., Cong Rec, Vol. 129, August 17, 1983, p. E4166.

The goals and accomplishments of King are discussed and the impact he had on the Civil Rights Movement.

1225 U.S. Congress, House. Representative William Moorhead speaking for "A Gold Medal to Honor Rev. Martin Luther King, Jr." 90th Cong., 2nd Sess., Cong Rec, Vol. 114, June 12, 1968, p. E17023.

Introduces a bill that would award a gold medal to the widow of Dr. King.

1226 U.S. Congress, House. Representative William S. Moorhead remarks on "Gold Medal Appropriate Tribute to Memory of Reverend Dr. Martin Luther King, Jr." 91st Cong., 1st Sess., Cong Rec, Vol. 115, January 15, 1969, p. E962.

Proposes that King be honored with a gold medal to recognize his outstanding contributions to the nation.

1227 U.S. Congress, House. Representative Robert Nix remarks on "Commerative Stamp Honoring the Life and Death of Dr. Martin Luther." 91st Cong., 1st Sess., Cong Rec, Vol. 115, April 14, 1969, pp. E8932-8933.

Questions the postal officials on the status of his request to have a stamp issued honoring Dr. King.

1228 U.S. Congress, House. Representative Henry J. Nowak commends "Talking Proud in Buffalo, NY." 97th Cong., 1st Sess., Cong Rec, Vol. 127, January 22, 1981, pp. E105-107.

Applauds the citizens of Buffalo on the events held honoring the death of the late Dr. King and endorsing his birthdate as a national holiday.

1229 U.S. Congress, House. Representative J. O'Hara remarks on "Funeral of Martin Luther King." 90th Cong., 2nd Sess., Cong Rec, Vol. 114, April 10, 1968, H9532.

Comments on the Congressmen in attendance at King's funeral and the other participants in the funeral service.

1230 U.S. Congress, House. Representative Thomas P. O'Neill, Jr. remarks on "A Man for All Seasons and All People." 90th Cong., 2nd Sess, Cong Rec, Vol. 114, April 10, 1968, p. H9654.

A Cardinal and the Mayor of Boston comments on the character and contributions of King to the Civil Rights Movement.

1231 U.S. Congress, House. Representative Thomas P. O'Neill, Jr. remarks on "The World We Must Share." 90th Cong., 2nd Sess., Cong Rec, Vol. 114, May 15, 1968, pp. E13557-13558.

Includes the text of a speech by a high school senior honoring and eulogizing the death of Dr. King.

1232 U.S. Congress, House. Representative William R. Rotchford speaking for "A Day of Remembrance for Dr. King." H.R. 800, 97th Cong., 2nd Sess., Cong Rec, Vol. 128, February 9, 1982, pp. E316-317.

Urges the House to take action on the bill that would make King's birthday a national holiday.

1233 U.S. Congress, House. Representative Ogden R. Reid remarks on "The First Martin Luther King Scholarships." 90th Cong., 2nd Sess., Cong Rec, Vol. 114, June 20, 1968, p. E18104.

A King scholarship is established by Mr. an Mrs. Bundschuh, Jr.

1234 U.S. Congress, House. Representative M. J. Rinaldo speaking for "Rev. Dr. Martin Luther King's Birthday." 98th Cong., 1st Sess., Cong Rec, Vol. 129, August 4, 1983, E4057.

Rinaldo hails those members of the House that voted for making King's birthday a national holiday.

1235 U.S. Congress, House. Representative P. Rodino speaking for "Dr. Martin Luther King, Jr., Recognition Day Program." 97th Cong., 2nd Sess., Cong Rec, Vol. 128, March 8, 1982, p. E792.

Discussion of a recognition program promoting the teachings of King.

1236 U.S. Congress, House. Representative P. Rodino speaking "To Designate the Birthday of Martin Luther King, Jr. as a Legal Public Holiday." 93rd Cong., 1st Sess., Cong Rec, Vol. 119, March 1, 1973, p. H6051.

Reintroduces a bill that would designate the birthday of King a national holiday.

1237 U.S. Congress, House. Representative Ryan speaking for "Martin Luther King's Birthday - January 15 - Should Be a National Holiday." 91st Cong., 2nd Sess., Cong Rec, Vol. 116, January 21, 1970, pp. H-615-616.

Calls for King's birthday to be made a national holiday and includes a copy of his "Letter from a Birmingham Jail."

1238 U.S. Congress, House. Representative W. Ryan speaking for "Martin Luther King, Jr. Day." 92nd Cong., 2nd Sess., Cong Rec, Vol. 118, January 19, 1972, p. H371.

Maintains that a permanent holiday for King would act as a reminder for future generations of his accomplishments in the field of civil rights.

1239 U.S. Congress, House. Representative Richard Schweiker remarks on "Moving Tribute to Dr. King by Pittsburgh Youth." 90th Cong., 2nd Sess., Cong Rec, Vol. 114, April 9, 1968, pp. E9344-9345.

Includes a poem from a high school student written in memory of the late Dr. King.

1240 U.S. Congress, House. Representative Gerry Sikorski speaking for "Dr. King Holiday New Sign of Hope." 98th Cong., 1st Sess., Cong

Rec, Vol. 129, October 24, 1983, p. E5080.

Contains an article calling for a holiday honoring Dr. King.

1241 U.S. Congress, House. Representative John Tuney remarks on "Baseball Tribute Through East-West All-Star Major League Classic to memory, Goals and Projects of Dr. Martin Luther King, Jr." 91st Cong., 2nd Sess., Cong Rec, Vol. 116, July 23, 1970, pp. E25696-2699.

Comments on the success of the baseball game held in honor of Dr. King and mentions a brief chronological account of his life with the civil rights movement.

1242 U.S. Congress, House. Representative J. Waldie comments on "Why Did They Kill martin Luther King, Jr.?" 91st Cong., 1st Sess., Cong Rec, Vol. 115, July 9, 1969, pp. H18817-18818.

Includes a speech written by a high school student on the life of Dr. King.

1243 U.S. Congress, House. Representative Ted Weiss speaking for "House Concurrent Resolution 153." H. Con. Res. 153, 97th Cong., 1st Sess., Cong Rec, Vol. 127, September 18, 1981, p. E4314.

Gives reasons for support of a resolution that would establish a statue of King in the Capitol.

1244 U.S. Congress, House. Representative Andrew Young remarks on "America Honors Dr. King." 93rd Cong., 1st Sess., Cong Rec, Vol. 119, February 7, 1973, pp. E5887-3888.

Comments on the anniversary celebration for Dr. King's birthday and the tribute that was held in support by the King Center for Social Change.

1245 U.S. Congress, Senate. Senator H. Baker speaking for consideration of "Martin Luther King, Jr. Holiday." H.R. 3706, 98th Cong., 1st Sess., Cong Rec, Vol. 129, October 3, 1983, pp. S13448-13469.

Covers hearings for and against recognition of a holiday honoring Dr. King. Several debates involve costs of such a holiday.

1246 U.S. Congress, Senate. Senator E. Brooke speaking for "Martin Luther King Day." 91st Cong., 1st Sess, Cong Rec, Vol. 115, January 15, 1969, p. S866.

Introduces a resolution that would set aside one day each year to commemorate the good deeds of Dr. King.

1247 U.S. Congress, Senate. Senator E. Brooke speaking for "Martin Luther King, Jr." 93rd Cong., 1st Sess., Cong Rec, Vol. 119, January 16, 1973, p. S1197.

Reintroducing a resolution that would make King's birthday a national holiday.

1248 U.S. Congress, Senate. Senator Edward Brooke remarks on "Recognition of Martin Luther King, Jr." 91st Cong., 2nd Sess., Cong Rec, Vol. 116, January 27, 1970, p. E1414.

Includes a poetic tribute to the late Dr. King.

1249 U.S. Congress, Senate. Senator Brooke speaking for "Senate Joint Resolution 159." 90th Cong., 2nd Sess., Cong Rec, Vol. 114, April 8, 1968, p. S9227.

Contends that King's birthday should be honored by all Americans each January.

1250 U.S. Congress, Senate. Senator T. Dodd speaking for "Martin Luther King, Jr." 97th Cong., 1st Sess., Cong Rec, Vol. 127, January 15, 1981, p. S200.

Hopes that this would be the year that legislators would enact a bill making King's birthday a national holiday.

1251 U.S. Congress, Senate. Senator East Criticizes "The Proposed Martin Luther King Holiday." 98th Cong., 1st Sess., Cong Rec, Vol. 129, September 20, 1983, p. S12556.

Urges the members of the Senate to vote against a holiday honoring King and presents several editorials that speak against a federal holiday for King.

1252 U.S. Congress, Senate. Senator B. Goldwater opposes "Martin Luther King, Jr. Holiday." H.R. 3706, 98th Cong., 1st Sess., Cong Rec, Vol. 129, October 3, 1993, pp. S13447-13448.

Opposition is given to the holiday because of the cost involved and the fact that King's contributions need further examination.

1253 U.S. Congress, Senate. Senator R. Griffin speaking for "S.1776 - Introduction of a Bill for the Issuance of a Special Postage Stamp in the Honor of the Late Dr. Martin Luther King, Jr." 91st Cong., 1st Sess., Cong Rec, Vol. 115, April 3, 1969, pp. S8603-8604.

1254 U.S. Congress, Senate. Senator F. Harris comments on "The Late Dr. Martin Luther King." 90th Cong., 2nd Sess., Cong Rec, Vol. 114, August 2, 1968, p. S24945.

A high school student pays tribute to the late Dr. King.

1255 U.S. Congress, Senate. Senator P. Hart speaking for "Tribute to Rev. Martin Luther King." 88th Cong., 1st Sess., Cong Rec, Vol. 109, July 2, 1963, pp. S12068-12069.

Bishop Emrich praises Dr. King for his use of nonviolence as a means of bringing about racial justice in America.

1256 U.S. Congress, Senate. Senator Vance Hartke remarks on "A

Memorial Sermon in Tribute to Rev. Dr. Martin Luther King, Jr." 90th Cong., 2nd Sess., Cong Rec, Vol. 114, April 17, 1968, p. E9924.

Submits the text of a sermon by Rev. Winters honoring the death of Dr. King.

1257 U.S. Congress, Senate. Senator F. Haskell speaking for "Senate Joint Resolution 20." 93rd Cong., 1st Sess., Cong Rec, Vol. 119, February 6, 1973, p. S3469.

This resolution recognize King's birthday as a day of celebration.

1258 U.S. Congress, Senate. Senator H. Humphrey speaking for "Dr. Martin Luther King, Jr." 93rd Cong., 1st Sess., Cong Rec, Vol. 119, January 12, 973, p. S1039.

Contains a letter written to the widow of Dr. King celebrating the forty-forth anniversary of his birth.

1259 U.S. Congress, Senate. Senator Humphrey for "Martin Luther King birthplace." 92nd Cong., 1st Sess., Cong Rec, Vol. 117, June 3, 1971, pp. S17757-17758.

Requests that Dr. King's birthplace become a national historic site.

1260 U.S. Congress, Senate. Senator J. Javits speaking for "Funeral Services for Dr. Martin Luther King." 90th Cong., 2nd Sess., Cong Rec, Vol. 114, April 10, 1968, pp. S9446-9448.

Eulogies paying tribute to Dr. King by DeWolfe an Rev. English are given.

1261 U.S. Congress, Senate. Senator E. Kennedy speaking for "House concurrent Resolution 153 Authorizing a Bust or Statue of Dr. Martin Luther King, Jr. to be Placed in the Capitol." H. Con. Res. 153, 97th Cong., 2nd Sess., Cong Rec, Vol. 128, December 21, 1982, p. S15925.

Commends the members of the Senate on the passage of the resolution establishing that a bust of King was to be placed in the Capitol.

1262 U.S. Congress, Senate. Senator G. McGovern speaking for "S743 - Introduction of a Bill to Designate Martin Luther King, Jr.'s Birthday as a National Day of Dedication." 92nd Cong., 1st Sess., Cong Rec, Vol. 117, February 10, 1971, S2468.

Gives reasons as to why King's birthday should become a national holiday.

1263 U.S. Congress, Senate. Senator C. Mathias speaking for "Dr. Martin Luther King, Jr." 97th Cong., 2nd Sess., Cong Rec, Vol. 128, December 21, 1982, pp. S15889-15890.

Salutes all those who helped to establish a bust of King in the halls of Congress.

1264 U.S. Congress, Senate. Senator J. Pearson comments on "Poems by Marguerite Mitchell Marshall." 91st Cong., 1st Sess., Cong Rec, Vol. 115, January 15, 1969, p. S909.

Includes two poems that pay homage to Dr. King.

1265 U.S. Congress, Senate. Senator C. Percy speaking for "Martin Luther King Holiday Bill." 98th Cong., 1st Sess., Cong Rec, Vol. 129, September 23, 1983, p. S12868.

The National Black Republican council passes a resolution calling for the approval of King's birthday as a national holiday.

1266 U.S. Congress, Senate. Senator D. Riegle speaking for "The Martin Luther King, Jr. Holiday." 98th Cong., 1st Sess., Cong Rec, Vol. 129, October 21, 1983, p. S14497.

Praises the passage of the bill to make King's birthday a national holiday.

1267 U.S. Congress, Senate. Senator P. Sarbanes speaking for "Martin Luther King, Jr. Holiday Bill." 98th Cong., 1st Sess., Cong Rec, Vol. 129, August 4, 1983, p. S11837.

Members of the House are commended for their passage of a bill honoring King, and the Senator asks that the Senate move in the same direction.

1268 U.S. Congress, Senate. Senator W. Scott speaking for "Dr. Martin Luther King, Jr. - Tribute by Senator Goodell." 91st Cong., 1st Sess., Cong Rec, Vol. 115, April 3, 1969, pp. S8664-8665.

Requests that April 4th of each year be set aside as a special day of appreciation to honor Dr. King.

1269 U.S. Congress, Senate. Senator W. Scott speaking for "S.3521 - Introduction of Bill to Provide for the Striking of Rev. Dr. Martin Luther King, Jr. Medals." 90th Cong., 2nd Sess, Cong Rec, Vol. 114, May 21, 1968, p. S14189.

Seeks the passage of a bill that would provide a gold medal to Mrs. King and duplicate bronze medals for public sale.

1270 U.S. Congress, Senate. Senator Scott speaking for "S. 3354 - Introduction of Bill to Authorize the Coinage of 50-Cent Pieces in Honor of Rev. Dr. Martin Luther King, Jr." 90th Cong., 2nd Sess., Cong Rec, Vol. 114, April 22, 1968, pp. S10114-10115.

The coin will pay tribute to King for his outstanding contribution to the civil rights movement and society.

1271 U.S. Congress, Senate. Senator Scott speaking for "S.3643 - Introduction of a Bill to Present to Coretta King a Gold Medal in

Honor and Commemoration of the life of the Reverend Dr. Martin Luther King, Jr." 91st Cong., 2nd Sess., Cong Rec, Vol. 116, March 26, 1970, pp. S9548-9549.

1272 U.S. Congress, Senate. Senator Ralph Yarborough speaking for "The Funeral Service of Dr. Martin Luther King, Jr. in Atlanta, GA." 90th Cong., 2nd Sess., Cong Rec, Vol. 14, May 27, 1968, pp. E15169-14172.

The complete order of the funeral service of King is given along with the complete eulogy by Benjamin Mays.

1273 FBI Headquarters Files. Birthday Commemoration for Martin Luther King, Jr. January 15, 1970, Washington, D.C.: FBI Headquarters Murkin Security Files, 1 p. (Mem. No. 3699).

Outlines information regarding planned activities to observe King's birthday.

1274 FBI Headquarters Files. Martin Luther King, Jr. - Racial Matters. August 27, 1969, Washington, D.C.: FBI Headquarters Murkin Security Files, 1 p. (Mem. No. 3670).

The Postmaster General requests information concerning King from the FBI as a basis on whether or not to issue a commemorative stamp on him.

1275 FBI Headquarters Files. Martin Luther King, Jr. Security Matter, February 25, 1969, Washington, D.C.: FBI Headquarters Murkin Security Files, 2 p. (Mem. No. 3728).

The Bureau contemplates whether it would be feasible to encourage Senators and Congressmen to oppose legislation on a bill making King's birthday a legal holiday.

1276 FBI Headquarters Files. Southern Christian Leadership Conference. January 23, 1969, Washington, D.C.: FBI Headquarters Murkin Security Files, 2 p. (Encl. No. 3560).

Demonstrations were held by SCLC honoring King's death and urging Congress to make his birthday a legal holiday.

1277 FBI Headquarters Files. Washington King Holiday - Committee. January 5, 1971, Washington, D.C.: FBI Headquarters Murkin Security Files, 5 p. (Encl. No. 3871).

Reveals the formulation of a committee that would work for the establishment of King's birthday as a national holiday.

Name Index

Includes authors and joint authors
Numbers refer to entry numbers.

Subject Index

Numbers refer to entry numbers.

Title Index

This index only includes material in the 1st 24 pages of this work

About the Compiler

SHERMAN E. PYATT is Assistant Professor and Serials/ Documents Librarian at The Citadel in Charleston, South Carolina.